YOU'RE WHAT YOU SENSE

D1554472

A Buddhianscientific
Dialogue on Mindbody

Ven. Bhikkhu Mihita, PhD

Pariyatti Press
an imprint of
Pariyatti Publishing
www.pariyatti.org

First published, 2001
Pariyatti edition, 2024

ISBN 978-1-68172-646-5 (paperback)
ISBN 978-1-68172-649-6 (PDF)
ISBN 978-1-68172-647-2 (ePub)
ISBN 978-1-68172-648-9 (Mobi)
Library of Congress Control Number: 2024931071

Cover image credits: Einstein graphic by dlsdkcgl at pixabay.com, Buddha statue and atom image designed by Freepik.com, skeleton graphic from reusableart.com.

Contents

The Basis for

BUDDHIANSCIENCE

Svākkhāto bhagavatā dhammo sandiṭṭhiko akāliko
ehi passiko opanayiko paccattaṃ veditabbo viññūhī'ti

Well explained

is the Dharma of the Exalted One,
a here and now,
timeless,
a come and see,
introspective,

and to be personally experienced by the wise.

... Kalamas, do not be led by reports, or tradition, or hearsay.
Be not led by the authority of religious texts, nor by mere logic
or inference, nor by considering appearances, nor by the delight
in speculative opinions, nor by seeming possibilities, nor by the
idea, 'this is our teacher'. But, O Kalamas, when you know for
yourselves ...[1]

---

1.   Saṃyutta Nikāya, Dhajaggaparitta Sutta; Aṅguttara Nikāya,
      p.115.

Preface

Buddha is known as a religious teacher, which, of course, he is. But few pay attention to his methodology—that his teachings were arrived at, what could only be called, scientifically, i.e., through a strict objectivity. Over six years leading up to his Enlightenment, what he did was to train his mind to be free from attachment—not only to the world but even to concepts (*paññatti*) and views (*diṭṭhi*) of any kind as well. The result of such fine-tuning of the *introscope* of his mind was total objectivity, a level a scientist could only envy.

It is in this objectivity that the Buddha declared that the only reality of the world, for a given individual, is what one gets through the senses, including the mind-sense, and senses alone, and indeed that you are what you sense.

If one finds spiritual comfort in the Buddha's teachings, I will have been humbled if these pages provide you with some scientific comfort as well, the two being, for the Buddha, not mutually exclusive. Those who are looking for his scientific concepts, I have boxed them for easy identification, and listed them all together at the end.

The dialogue format you'll encounter here was taken from the Buddha himself. It is used not only to keep the presentation lighthearted, but also to impart the idea that the study of Buddhism can be joyous. If you find the Enquirer in the dialogue interjecting with "I see", "Yes", "I agree", "Mh" and the like, it is partly to maintain the flow of conversation. But it is also to continue an early tradition, perhaps best retained among the Sinhalese Buddhists. Listening to a discourse, at a temple or home setting, you'll find a senior member of the congregation respond, from time to time, with phrases like '*ehey*' (respectfully) yes, '*ehemay*' indeed (respectfully) yes', sometimes addressing the 'respected teacher' (*swaamin vahansa*). It is as if to assure that the listeners were all ears (even though some may well be half-asleep, particularly if the event is held in the night!).

My thanks go to Ven. Wimalajoti, Director of the Buddhist Cultural Centre and his staff for an excellent job done in a very short time. My love goes to Swarna, without whose unstinting support and continuing care this book would never have been written.

May you be well, and happy!

Suwanda H. J. Sugunasiri, PhD
University of Toronto &
Nalanda College of Buddhist Studies
August 2001

Preface to the Second Edition

It is with pleasure that I write this brief Preface to the second edition of *You're What You Sense*, a work on Abhidhamma 'metaphysics', drawn upon the ancient treatment *Abhidhammatthasangaha*. While today literature on Buddhadhamma is rich in the English medium, material on Abhidhamma is still rare.

When this book was initially published in 2001, it was said to be a best seller at the exit lounge of an international airport. What this seems to suggest is that the work was attractive to the western reader. One reason for this may be the informal dialogical style in which the book is written, reminding the knowledgeable reader of the dialogue between the Greek King Menander and Venerable Nagasena. But another may be that the enjoyment takes the reader to a deeper understanding of the Buddhadhamma. A third may be that the study draws upon Westernscientific concepts, this by way of clarifying a concept in a scientific, i.e., objective, manner as allowed by the content. And the light that shines upon them from this reaching out may be how Buddhadhamma is no archaic teaching but very much modern, indeed even going beyond what is known in the West.

So I thank Mr. Brihas Sarathy of Pariyatti Publishing for his critical decision to undertake this 2nd edition, to make the Buddhadhamma available for a wider North American audience, in the context of more and more people looking to be guided by the wisdom and compassion of the Buddha.

I thank Mr. Steve Hanlon of the publishing department, and his associates, for resetting the layout and correcting a few errors in the first edition.

May you be well and happy!

Ven. Bhikkhu Mihita
January 2024

List of Figures

Setting the Context

Interested in Buddha's teachings, you, the enquirer (E), have asked me (M), a student of Buddhism, to talk to you about the make-up of your mindbody from a Buddhist point of view. You have obviously come with a vague idea of Buddhism, and you fit the description 'the average well-educated'. In response, I invite you to a dialogue, the Buddha having used dialogue as an effective tool of communication with many an enquirer who came to him.

DIALOGUE ONE

YOU'RE A MINDBODY, PLAIN & SIMPLE!

The contingent nature of the self—and the consequent spaciousness and workability of experience—is, ... grounded in the radical interdependence of all phenomena, set forth in the Buddha's central doctrine of causality, ... or dependent co-arising. In this doctrine, which the Buddha equated with the Dharma, ... everything arises through mutual conditioning in reciprocal interaction. Indeed the very word Dharma conveys not a substance or essence, but orderly process itself—the way things work.

Joanna Macy, *Mutual Causality in Buddhism and General Systems Theory*[2]

---

2.   Macy, Preface, p. xi.

1.1 No Form, No Eye

M. So you want to know who you are?

E. Yeah... Increasingly, I seem to be intrigued by the question "Who am I?". So I'd like to get a good handle on it.

M. Sounds like a sensible query. I'll try my best.

E. I'm sure you will.

M. So are you then ready?

E. As ready as ever!

M. What if I were to then tell you that you're, in one word, a *mindbody*!

E. A mindbody? How do you mean?

M. Well, when you just asked me a question, you used your *body*—mouth and tongue, for instance, and eye contact, gestures, etc. But before you opened your mouth, you had to put your brain process in gear.

E. I certainly can't disagree.

M. Well... So that is your *mind...* .

E. You mean the conceptualization and all that?

M. Yes. By 'all that', of course, you mean the automatic process of looking for the right sentence or question, the best words—or put another way, the sounds and the appropriate sound sequence, the emotions associated with them, how respectful or disrespectful you were going to be, the suitable distance you were going to maintain with the speaker, and so on.

E. You mean everything that makes for good communication.

M.   Yes. Now for the Buddha, mind is only one of three 'doors.' *Body* and *word* are the other two.

E.   Oh, you mean *mind*, *body* and *word* are the channels through which we express ourselves.

M.   Exactly. Not only express, but also process information.

E.   Well, of course.

⚛ *Scientific Concepts*

1.1   **Mind, body and word: the three doors through which info is outputted and inputted.**

M.   Now, if this single act of speaking makes you a mindbody, a mindbody in action, everything we do through the three doors, then, make you, and me, and everyone else, mindbodies!

E.   Oh, that's what you mean by mindbody. I see. But, tell me something here. Why mindbody, and not bodymind? Is there a special reason?

M.   Believe you me, there is a very good reason. In fact, you already know it!

E.   I do?

M.   Indeed! Let me ask you, where is the thinking? In the mind or in the body?

E.   Well, I'd say mind... .

M.   Dead on! In the world according to the Buddha, it is the *mind* that is primary and supreme. Here're the classic lines from the *Dhammapada*.

E.   *Dhammapada*? What's that?

M.   Oh, it's a collection of some of the Buddha's nifty sayings. It's so popular that there are several English translations of it.

E. Perhaps I should look one up. But let's hear the lines.

M. *Mind is first off the mark, leading all the way,*
   and mind-made everything is.
   If one speaks or acts with an evil mind,
   misery stalks one as surely as
   those cart-wheels the yoked bull!

   Mind is first off the mark, leading all the way,
   and mind-made everything is.
   If one speaks or acts with a good mind,
   happiness leaves you not, as surely as
   the shadow that deserts you not! [3]

E. Interesting similes.

M. Oh yes, the Buddha was a maestro in the art of language use—similes, metaphors, analogies, narratives, tales. You name it, he has it!

E. I bet.

M. Now "*mind is first off the mark*" is simply to remind us that at the back of what's called 'I', 'me' or 'you' is the mind.

E. I get it.

 *Scientific Concepts*

1.2   Everything in being human begins with the mind.

M. So having a mind, or to talk of it by another of its names, sense, is what makes the difference between, say, a rock—with no mind, or sense—and a sentient being.

E. Sentient being?

M. Yes, that's the Buddha's collective term for a human being or animal. Just to make the point that they're both made up of senses.

---

3.   Dhammapada, Book I, verse 1.

E. Makes sense... So animals fall into the same category as humans.

M. Yes, siree!

> ⚛ *Scientific Concepts*
>
> *1.3* *Sentient being: one with senses.*
> *1.4* *Sentient being: both humans and animals come under the same class.*

E. Darwin would be delighted to hear that a religious teacher puts both animals and humans in the same class.

M. I'm sure Buddha would've loved his company! The more so because Buddha calls himself an analyst.

E. Certainly looks like one, from the little we've talked so far.

M. Let's, then, imagine you're about to leave home for work, and are standing in front of a mirror to take that last look before you head out. Sure, you see how smartly dressed you're and all that... But if you took the time, and took a careful look at your body, what do you see?

E. My face.

M. Only?

E. My eyes, ears, nose?

M. And a whole *body*, right?

E. Right...

M. And if you opened your mouth, there'd be the tongue.

E. Yes. So what's special about that?

M. Nothing! As a list, this is nothing more than sticking labels. But you tell me, when we finish our conversation, whether there is anything special in the Buddha's understanding of it all, his taxonomy if you like.

E.   OK.

M.   Let me then make the startling assertion that you had to have your eyes *open* to see all these body parts in the mirror! How's that for a shocker? Seriously, behind that simple assertion is a profound basis for our understanding of how our senses work... Or indeed what a 'sense' means... .

E.   Let's hear it.

M.   You know from your Psychology 101 that for you to see, the image of your body has to fall on your physical eye. For that to happen, it has to be open, of course. It is, in fact, on the retina that the image falls, which as you know, is connected to the nerve endings within the brain through the optic nerve.

E.   Wait a minute, wait a minute ... but what's all this got to do with the Buddha?

M.   Glad you asked. He calls the physical eye the *composite eye*. It's 'composite' because it includes more than one component. The *sensitive eye* is one of them, and it is described as set in '*the black circle surrounded by the white*' and lying '*where the shadow of the stimulus falls*.

E.   Intriguing! So according to the Buddha, the stimulus comes to the eye. Isn't that the very opposite of what the Greeks thought? Their understanding was that the eye goes to the stimulus.

M.   Yes. Buddha clearly didn't think that.

E.   That's fantastic. It was not until a few centuries ago that even western science understood it that way.

M.   That's my understanding, too.

E.   So Buddha was ahead of western science by well over two millennia. O' gosh!

M. Looks that way, doesn't it? But to get back to where we were at, the sensitive eye is characterized as set in 'where the shadow of the stimulus falls.' So what do you think that is?

E. Retina?

M. Bull's eye! That's what it appears to me, too. And it's said to spread '*like a drop of oil that pervades seven membranes made of cotton*'.

E. Buddha says this?

M. Aha! Then there's the *eye-door-path* along which, say, a light that falls on the retina travels.

E. Oh, the optic nerve?

M. Exactly... And so, eventually, there's the resulting **eye sense,** *or* eye-mind, or to give the more familiar term, *eye-consciousness.*

E. Wow! Buddha explains it in all that detail?

M. You bet! So *composite eye*, then, is basically the retina and the optic nerve put together.

E. But including I suppose other parts like the lens, the iris, and so on.

 *Scientific Concepts*

1.5 *Composite eye = sensitive eye (retina) + eye-door path (optic nerve).*

M Yes. But what I found even more interesting is how the light, the external *stimulus itself comes to be part of eye-sense.*

E. Stimulus is part of consciousness? That seems strange. It's outside the body.

M. The Buddha's point, of course, is that there would be no 'seeing' if there was nothing to see. Let me explain with an example. Seen a butterfly lately?

E.   This past summer.

M.   Good.... Let's say you saw it at 6.23 PM as you were strolling in the park. At that point, it became part of *your* world. Since that time, you can see! it in your mind's eye—its colours, size, shape, etc.

E.   Yes, I have a very clear visual memory of it...yes.

M.   But before 6.23 PM *that day*, that butterfly wasn't part of *your* world. Not that it wasn't there before that, but that it was not a slice of your world.

E.   Never thought of it that way but I guess that's true.

M.   In fact, (a) had you not been there in the park that evening, and (b) that butterfly had not appeared in the path of your vision, it would still not be part of your world. So this is why we can say that the stimulus (the butterfly in this case) is very much part of your eye-consciousness. No butterfly, no butterfly consciousness for you!

E.   Funny, when you think of it, makes total sense...

M.   So Buddha's understanding is that while there is a world outside there, independent of us, it is not *your* world or *my* world until and unless you come into *contact* with it. On the other hand, what you see of that world through *your* own eye at a given point in and a given place *alone* is *your* world.

E.   Aha... So it's WYSIWYG, as in computer language   What You See Is What You Get!

M.   Interesting mnemonic tool alright. I'll have to remember it, too—WYSIWYG, right? So anyways, your face you see in the mirror, i.e., the stimulus, is part of your visual sense.

E.   Quite a revolutionary idea...

M.   Would seem that way, doesn't it?

E. Now, wouldn't it be interesting if we could find evidence for such an idea in modern science?

M. It certainly would be.

E. So is there?

M. You want to try the cellular level?

E. That might be quite interesting! Yes, that will be.

M. And this would not be far-fetched for Buddhist thought, because in fact, there's a term in the texts that can be translated as '*minute ball*'. I wouldn't want to call it an exact parallel to a cell. But it does suggest a physical form in a diminutive size.

E. Hm! Probably need a leap of faith here...

M. Which is actually not bad, in a sort of suspension of disbelief, like when you watch a movie, especially because the point being made does not hinge on it.

E. I guess.

M. Let's, then, see what a cell biologist has to say: *Signals and messages are carried by minute particles of matter... Thus, a photon striking a retinal cell will induce very slight reactions. When amplified by chemical processes, these reactions will eventually activate the entire receptor cell. This is one of the secrets of visual function that has been discovered at the cellular level.*[4]

E. Yeah, I can see the parallels—a photon striking a retina cell, activating the receptor cell and all that!

4. Kordan, p.24-5.

> **⚛ *Scientific Concepts***
>
> *1.6   Stimulus is part of consciousness.*
> *1.7   Eye-consciousness: result of an external stimulus*
> *falling on the retina and traveling along the optic*
> *nerve.*

M. Great! So then, there are three conditions that would result in, say, eye consciousness:

(1) a *stimulus;*

(2) a *physical eye*, that is both open and working; and

(3) a *sensitive* (or mental) *eye* (with 'eye-door-path', i.e., neural connections).

E. Mh...

M. Stimulus we've already talked about. We've asserted a part of number (3): a physical eye that's open. You wouldn't have seen your face in that mirror, or that butterfly, had you had your eyes closed.

E. Like in sleep you mean.

M. Yes, when we can't even see our own body! The other part of (2) is that there would be no seeing either if the eyes were not in *working order*. Helen Keller's mother ...you know Keller, don't you?

E. Who doesn't? Isn't that the American woman who went blind and deaf in infancy, but went on to be a great writer and lecturer, having being taught to speak and read.

M. That's her alright, yes. So when Helen's mom moved her hand and a bright lamp in front of Helen's eyes on that fateful day when she went blind, her eyes were open, and she was looking straight ahead, but she saw nothing!

E. Because her eyes were not working.

M. Exactly. Now number (2) is 'sensitive eye with neural connections'. We've talked about it, right?

E. Right.

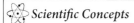 *Scientific Concepts*

1.8   Conditions for eye-consciousness:
a. stimulus,
b. open eye,
c. working eye,
d. and a sensitive (or mental) eye (with neural
    connections).

M. So far we've talked about just the one eye-consciousness. Let me now lay out the standard five senses, or *consciousness(es)* if you like, showing the three conditions for each. I'll list them under 'mind', 'body' and 'stimulus', reversing the order. Remember, mind comes first.

1	2	3	4
Type of Consciousness	**MIND**	**BODY**	**STIMULUS**
Visual Consciousness	sensitive eye	physical eye	form
Aural Consciousness	sensitive ear	physical ear	sound
Nasal Consciousness	sensitive nose	physical nose	smell
Lingual Consciousness	sensitive tongue	physical tongue	taste
Tactile Consciousness	sensitive body	physical body	touch

Figure 1A. The fivefold consciousness(es), showing the three conditions for the functioning of each

E. Looks like a neat schema. Could we go through it?

M. Well, column 1 is straightforward....

E. Yes, they are the five senses.

M. So you know it. Why ask me?

E.   Just testing ... to see if you know it!

M.   I concede defeat... So you want me to pack up and go?

E.   Of course, not! But let's see here. 'Stimulus' I understand, too. But you want to say something about 'mind' and 'body'?

M.   Remember we talked about the 'sensitive eye' and the 'physical eye'? We may remember how they work: (a) the electrical impulse of the ray of light that falls on the retina, (b) triggering a reaction and activating the optic nerve that carries it to the brain.

E.   Aha!

M.   But remember that they make up a *single* composite eye.

E.   Yes.

M.   That means that one has no separate existence from the other. They're shown separately in the chart to remind ourselves of the two aspects of a given sense.

E.   So that's what you mean by mind and body.

 **Scientific Concepts**

1.9   *Every form of consciousness is made up of three parts: mental, physical and stimular.*

M.   Yes.

E.   So then each of what you've listed as sensitive eye, ear.... to sensitive body, should be understood in terms of a double dimension.

M.   Purr...fect!

E.   So basically at the back of the physical eye, physical ears, etc. is a psychological process.

M.   Right. And guess who agrees.

E.   Who?

M.   Do you know the Human Genome Project?

E.   Isn't that the one that's trying to figure out the makeup of our genetic machine, the scientific basis of our DNA?

M.   You got it.

E.   So what about it?

M.   Well, in a book by one of its leading figures, there's a chapter titled, "*All in the mind*". [5]

E.   Interesting!

M.   He's tracing the advances in our understanding of the human genetic structure. In the process he points to "*the myriad illnesses [such as schizophrenia, manic depression, alcoholism, senile dementia...] that are produced when the mind malfunctions*". [6]

E.   So the idea is that the workings of the mind is at the back of our health or ill-health.

M.   Indeed.

E.   I wonder what the Buddha would have to say about that.

M.   Why don't you ask him the next time you meet him!

E.   Now that's a thought. But where will I find him?

M.   Oh, that's easy. Look within.

E.   Just like that, eh? Ouw Kay! I'll keep my eyes open.

M.   Good, and good luck.

E.   Gee, thanks!

---

5.   Bodmer & McKie, pp.125ff.

6.   Bodmer & McKie, p.126.

NOTES, REFLECTIONS & QUERIES

1.2 No Mind, No Matter

M. Now, do you find anything missing in the schemata?

E. Let me see now.... There's the eye, ear, nose, tongue and body... Hey, wait a minute! Where's the mind here?

M. You're sharp! The Buddha indeed does talk of a sixth sense.

E. You mean, there is yet another sense coming soon to a body near you!

M. Nicely put!

E. And what would that be called?

M. The mind sense, or mind consciousness.

E. Mind consciousness?

M. Yes. Foundational to the other five senses.

E. So the mind sense is at the back of these other senses. I can live with it.

M. Yes, but this is only one of its functions.

E. And its other function?

M. Are you ready for it?

E. Go!

M. Let me show it along the same dimension as with the other senses (see Figure 1B).

TYPE	MIND	BODY	STIMULUS
MIND CONSCIOUSNESS	*sensitive mind*	*physical mind*	*mental constructs*

Figure 1B. The Three Conditions of Mind Consciousness

E.   Boggles ma mind, I'll tell ya!

M.   If it's any comfort, I struggled with it, too, for the longest time before it made sense to me.

E.   Yeah. It's very confusing!

M.   Let me try to make things clearer. Well, did you understand the three conditions for eye-consciousness—the sensitive eye, the physical eye and the stimulus.

E.   That was alright.

M.   How about in relation to the other four?

E.   That was alright, too.

M.   So I'm trying to capture the same idea when it comes to the mind sense. There's a mental base (sensitive mind), a physical base (physical mind) and a stimulus (mental constructs).

E.   I follow your logic, but I sure don't know what the dickens 'sensitive mind' or the 'physical mind' is! You want to say a bit more?

M.   Sure. The *physical mind* would be the total nervous system— the brain with its neurons, spinal cord, and other related physical parts.

E.   OK... And the *sensitive mind*.

M.   The psychological process, for example, of the communication that takes place within the nervous system.

E. You mean ... let me think through this... Is it something like the brain telling us to move away from an oncoming vehicle or taking in the music at a concert?

M. Great examples!

E. But the sensitive and the physical mind, as you said earlier, have no independent existence.

M. You get the idea. Yes. So perhaps we ought to think of, if you like, a 'composite mind'.

E. You mean, like the composite eye, made up of different parts.... Yeah, that might work.

M. But let's return to the *sensitive mind*. At the point of conception, there would obviously be only the mind sense.

E. Because the other five have not evolved as yet?

M. Exactly. So the sensitive mind has only one function at this earliest stage of life: *to be foundational to itself*!

E. Hm. Foundational to itself... foundational to itself!

M. Well, it's complicated enough all right. But perhaps we might get a handle on this if we go to the cellular level again.

E. Am I ready for this?

M. Sure you are! We know that at the point of conception, all we have is a single cell—no eye, no ear, no nose, no tongue— that we can write home about!

E. OK.

M. Why don't we, in fact, look at a cell diagram?

E. That's a great idea.

M. So here it is.

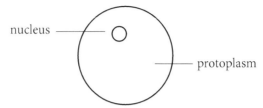

Figure 1C. A Cell showing its two main parts, a Nucleus (enclosed within a membrane) and the Protoplasm (within a cell wall)

E.   I certainly see no eyes or mouth here?

M.   Wow! Your powers of observation are phenomenal!!

E.   Well, I don't want to flag it...

M.   Yes, I can see humility written all over your face.

E.   What can I say?

M.   So anyways, it is only after a few weeks that the eyes and other senses begin to appear, right?

E.   Right.

M.   Yet there is life, wouldn't you say, in that single cell.

E.   Indeed. Otherwise it can't divvy up and grow.

M.   There you're! So, of the six senses, all we have in that first cell is only the mind sense. By definition. Fair enough?

E.   Fair enough!

M.   So because we've identified the mind to be 'composite', there has to be in that cell both parts of the 'composite mind'—the sensitive and the physical.

E.   Hm... Beginning to make sense. But can you say a little more.

M.   Well, here's a finding from genetics that may help us. "...*up to half our total complement* [*of genes*] *are thought to be involved in controlling brain function*".[7] If we accepted the view of western science that the brain is the seat of consciousness (we'll come to the Buddhist view later), we may say that half of the genes are involved in the functions of consciousness. Genes are, of course, chemical processes, more mind than matter. So can we not then say that the mind (=genes) is foundational to itself (=brain)?

E.   It's a stretch, but I suppose I can see the argument.

M.   Good. So now you understand the sense in which I say that the mind is foundational to itself.

E.   Yeah... sort of...

M.   OK, let's see if we can get some help from genetic studies.

E.   That's good enough for now!

M.   Later, of course, mind takes on the other function we've talked about.

E.   You mean being foundational to the other five senses.

M.   Yes.

E.   Now that I get. And you know what? Complicated as it is, I believe I'm beginning to get the hang of it.

M.   Great! Perhaps everything may not be clear at this point, but will be later, believe you me, if you bear with me.

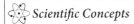 *Scientific Concepts*

1.10   *There are not five but six senses, the sixth being the mind sense.*

1.11   *Mind sense has two functions:*
        a. to be foundational to itself;
        b. to be foundational to the other five senses.

---

7.   Bodmer & McKie, p.126.

E. I sure hope so. But now that I have some sense of the sensitive and the physical mind, can you tell me more about 'mental constructs' in the last column?

M. You won't rest until you get the total picture, do you now! That's the spirit!!

E. Well, I came to find out.

M. Well, of course! So to continue, then, the Buddha's term for what I've called 'mental construct' is *dharma* (in Sanskrit) or *dhamma* (in Pali). It's a word with many meanings, depending on the context.[8] But here I mean... No, let me do a little experiment... You have your eyes open, and you see me in front of you... But now, close your eyes. Do you 'see' anything in your, er, mind's eye, so to speak?

E. Yes, of course. A picture of you...

M. Is this a mental image?

E   Yes.

M   That, then, is one thing that's meant by *dharma* here. A mental image, a mental construct, a thought...

E. I get it.

M. But let's continue our experiment. Can you go back to your childhood?

E. How far?

M. How far can you go?

E. Well, I can see myself running after a ball... barely though.

M   That's a memory, another *dharma*. Now let me ask you. Oh, you may open your eyes. You love democracy, don't you? But can you put your finger on it and show it out to me?

---

8.   Watanabe, pp.9-17.

E.   Well... no... but I know what it means.

M.   So it's not something you can touch or feel. Yet you have pretty good idea of what that means. It's a 'concept'. Well, there's another *dharma* for ya!

E.   So there are several meanings.

M.   Yes... Have you ever caught yourself saying, "Oh, I think". That's something you've created yourself, brand new, hot off the press, I mean, hot off the brain! That, too, is a *dharma*.

E.   OK.

M.   Seen a mirage?

E.   Yep.

M.   That's a *dharma*, too, even though it's a false construct of your mind. Then there are dreams, aspirations, wishes, etc., all creations of your mind, which may or may not have anything to do with reality or the world outside of you.

E.   So *dharma* means concepts, ideas and the like we've encountered and internalized.

M.   Or even never encountered but constructed by ourselves— novel and unique combinations.

E.   So how about creativity by artists, scientists, etc.

M.   Yes, they would be *dharma*, too.

E.   So it's a whole slew of things? Thoughts, ideas, abstract objects, goals...

M.   Even sentences, language...

E.   All right.

M.   But at the point when a sentient being is conceived, i.e., at that cellular level, this *dharma*, the mental construct, if you remember the third component of the mind-consciousness, may simply be something inchoate like, "I want to be", "I want to divvy up myself" and the like!

E.   That's funny!

M.   Yeah, but the point here is, and it's a difficult one, that the cell is there only because it wants to be. And it divides itself up only because it wants to replicate itself!

E.   Whaddaya mean? Too much for me! Too much.

M.   Oh, you're trying to be modest, I know. We'll come to the details of this fundamental idea in Buddha's teachings later when you read about the concept of craving, or more commonly, attachment (Figure 2C), but the general idea is simple enough. For instance, you came to see me because you wanted to see me, right?

E.   I can buy that.

M.   Or, you see something, say like a painting, and you decide to like it or dislike it.

E.   So you're saying that I like it or don't like it because I decided it that way? Hm! An interesting idea... Something to think about.

M.   OK, while you work on it, let me suggest another of the *dharmas*, another mental construct of that first cell: "I want to be nourished".

E.   But it's only a cell!

M.   True enough. But does it have life?

E.   In some sense, I suppose.

M.   Can there be life without nourishment?

E.   I guess not!

M. In fact, nourishment is one of the fundamental features of a cell. The other, of course, is 'motion'.[9] Remember divvying up?

E. Oh, so that's why you say the cell has this mental construct, this *dharma*, "I want nourishment".

M. Exactly. It wants nourishment.

E. I guess it makes sense.

M. You know what the Buddha calls it?

E. What?

M. He calls it *consciousness food*. It's 1 of 4 kinds of nourishment. Basically it means that consciousness feeds on itself for subsistence!

E. Ca...nni...ba...lis...tic!

M. You think so, eh. Well, we'll get a better understanding of it later, but for now, can we hang on to the idea of consciousness food?

E. For sure.

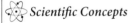 *Scientific Concepts*

1.12   *Consciousness food is one of four kinds of nourishment for a sentient being.*

M. Now you have a sense of the mind-sense. Like the other senses, then, it comes into existence only in the context of a stimulus. No stimulus, no mind. And if it isn't still all clear, don't worry, we'll return to it as we continue to explore.

E. I sure hope!

M. But in the meantime, let me draw your attention to the miracle of freezing a patient, for medical purposes, for up to 4 hours.

---

9.   Gray, p.2.

E.   Yeah. I read about it. Now isn't that amazing, when there's no heartbeat or brain functioning.

M.   Exactly. Yet, the patient can be brought back to her/his fully functioning senses after a full four hours. Of course, we can't revive a dead person the same way.

E.   So you're saying that the reason why a frozen human body can be returned to normal functioning is because there's a mind sense.

M.   Like I said, you're brilliant! Exactly. Clearly the five senses are gone. So something should be sustaining the life. And if, as we've understood so far, the six senses constitute life, what's left?

E.   Aha! The mind-sense! Beautiful.... Yeah, that would be suggestive of the presence of something other than the five senses. Great!

M.   Now we said that the mind-consciousness is foundational to itself. But later, that single cell blooms into a beautiful thingy we call the *embryo*, and then a *fetus*—with a shapely body, beautiful eyes, ears to pierce, nose to breathe through and a hanging tongue! And, behind that blooming is the mind-consciousness that becomes foundational to these other senses.

E.   Yes, I could well buy that now.

M.   To revisit the mind and the body as in Figures 1A and 1B, then, if mind is what we can't see with the naked eye, body is what we can. The Buddha uses the terms *nāma* and *rūpa*, literally 'name' and 'form' respectively for these two. We could call it 'psychological you' and 'physical you'. The two are opposite to, distinct from, each other in one sense, but complementary, too, in another. So to catch this latter sense, Buddha uses the composite term *nāmarūpa*, putting 'em together, to refer to a sentient being.

E.   *Nāmarūpa.* Mindbody!

M.   Yes... to mean that they are related to each other in a way that if one were to be absent, the other wouldn't be there either. In other words, *no matter no mind, no mind no matter!*

E.   You do like wordplay, don't you.

M.   Bread and butter of a writer!

E.   In any case, Descartes is wrong then.

M.   You mean where he sees an accidental, or contingent, relationship between the two?

E.   Yes, where you can have my body and I can have your mind!

M.   The Buddha, by contrast, sees a 'necessary relationship', a reciprocal one.

E.   And I can see where he's coming from.

M.   Wonderful! Now in *nāmarūpa*, we have the beginnings of you, me and all sentient beings.

E.   So a cell, too, would be a *nāmarūpa* then?

M.   Right on. For, as we said, at the point of conception of a human being, the single cell, with a nucleus and protoplasm, would be the total mindbody!

E.   So you're saying that there'd be no nucleus without the protoplasm and no protoplasm without the nucleus, right?

M.   Exactly. Now let me introduce you to another of Buddha's related concepts, a much misunderstood one.

E.   And that would be?

M.   That the mind is in the *whole body*—not in the heart as even Buddhist scholars over the last 2500 years have said.[10] His

---

10. Sugunasiri, 1995.

words are quite straightforward: '*conditioned by consciousness is mindbody; conditioned by mindbody is consciousness*'.

E. How do you mean?

M. Take breathing, for example. There'd be no outbreath if there's no inbreath.

E. And *verci vysa*... I mean, vice versa.

M. Exactly.

E. So Buddha is saying that if there's no consciousness, there's no body, and if there's no body, there's no consciousness.

M. Right on.

E. But what about a brain-dead person?

M. What about a brain-dead one?

E. Well brain-dead means no consciousness. Right?

M. Wrong. Brain-dead only means that some parts of the brain that controls brain function are dead. But since the brain-dead person continues to breathe, surely it would make sense to say that the part of the brain that controls breathing—assuming that the brain is the engine that drives all mindbody functions—can't be dead! As in the case of a frozen body.

E. Yeah, I can see that.

M. Remember the geneticist view that up to half our total complement of all our genes are thought to be involved in controlling brain function? This means that there're a whole lot of genes—nearly half—that control other functions.

E. That concurs with your explanation that brain-dead does not mean you're totally dead.

M. I rest my case.

E. So what you're saying is that as long as there's breathing, there's life.

M. Now you're talking. Since breathing is a physical activity, or 'body', we can say that mind, i.e., consciousness, ceases when the body ceases.

E. And, of course, vice versa, you would say.

M. And vice versa. Texts say that the two—mind and body—are co-emergent.

E. Co-emergent! Yeah, makes sense.

M. That's why we can say that if there's no consciousness, there's no body, and if there's no body, there's no consciousness.

E. So the relationship is reciprocal.

M. Right again.

⚛ *Scientific Concepts*

1.13 Consciousness is in the whole body.

1.14 The relationship between consciousness and mindbody is reciprocal.

E. Buddha's understanding of the mind is remarkable. And so modern. I'm thinking of what I read in *Psychology Today*[11] sometime ago.

M. What.

E. That the mind is in the whole body.

M. Exactly. Now don't we have a great team going here! Yes, the Buddha sees the mind in the whole body, but from head to toe only—not in your hair or finger nails.

E. Oh... you mean that's why I can cut them without going ouch!

---

11. John, 1976.

M.   Exactly.

>  *Scientific Concepts*
>
> **1.15   *The seat of consciousness is the whole body, except hair & nails.***

E.   I'm now beginning to understand why you said that I am a mindbody.

M.   Wonderful! So when I want to be fancy about it, can I call you a *psychophysique* instead of a mindbody, plain and simple? Let's get a little classy here, eh!

E.   Let's! Sometimes I like to feel important! My ego needs a little boost!

M.   Now watch it! You know that there's no such thing as an ego. Or soon you'll find out.

E.   Oh!

M.   Yes. Waiting for an ego will be like waiting for a piece of the sky to fall off. But that's for later.

E.   I can hardly wait!

NOTES, REFLECTIONS & QUERIES

1.3 Life Grows on a Tree

M. Let me now bring to your attention to a few more things regarding mindbody.

E. I'm ready.

M. OK then, what's ESP?

E. Even I know that! Extra-sensory Perception?

M. Good. Extra-sensory, by definition, means, outside of the senses, right? Like extra-marital, for example.

E. That's what it suggests certainly.

M. But I would argue that there is no such thing! I would argue that all perception is very much *sensory*, and sensory alone.

E. You want to tell me why.

M. We have seen (in Figure 1A) that there would be no visual perception, i.e., visual consciousness or simply 'seeing', without a stimulus, this in the form of shape, colour, intensity, distance, etc., falling upon the retina (physical condition). Likewise for the other four. We noted the same thing regarding the mind sense (Figure 1B). So we see that everything is sensory—based in a sense.

E. Hm... Everything is sensory! Nothing is extra-sensory. Great for a mantra!

M. Yes. I believe the misapprehension came about from the western idea of only five senses. But when it became increasingly apparent that there seem to be certain human experiences unexplainable purely in relation to the five senses, the creative solution was to suggest they were simply 'extra-sensory'!

E. Didn't it even come to be called the horse-sense.

M. Indeed. Little did western philosophy know that Indian thought had already named it as the mind, and come to recognize a sixth sense.

E. Oh, you mean, Brahminism.

M. Yes. The English word 'man' is not unrelated to the Pali/Sanskrit term *mano*, meaning 'mind'.

E. Interesting.

M. Understanding the human experience in terms of six senses alone, then, the Buddha lays out the inclusive idea in a nice little one-liner: '*In this one-fathom body I posit the world*'!

E. Fathom...?

M. ...about the length of your two arms outstretched.

E. Oh, is that what it is? I presume this was the unit of measurement of the time.

M. Right. So the one-liner basically tells us, for example, that if there were no smell around, you wouldn't be smelling anything. My world, to re-emphasize, then, is what I experience through my senses, and yours through your senses; nothing more, nothing less.

E. Ahem... That sure seems to be the case. So *ESP is a convenient myth*!

 *Scientific Concepts*

1.16 *Your world is nothing but your whole mindbody, nothing more, nothing less!*

1.17 *Nothing comes from nothing; i.e., all perception is sensory, or sense-based. Hence extra-sensory perception is a fiction.*

M. You got it. Now, of course, this world, of mine and yours, changes every nanosecond, or as the Buddha would say, every *mindmoment* (and we'll come to it shortly), but whatever world one has at any given point in time, it is still experienced through the senses. Makes sense?

E. Well, I cannot disagree.

M. But this also means that not only is your world what you make through your senses, but you *are* that world! Again, nothing more, nothing less. The outside world of the sun and the moon, of mice and men, of schools and hospitals, of books and television, and the like, of course, do exist, but unless you have encountered them through your own senses, they are not your world.

E. I'm sure Helen Keller would agree.

M. The picture of a Vancouver sunset, for example, is not part of Helen's world. Not mine either, as I write this. No wonder each of the ten blind people in the Buddhist folktale thought that each part of the elephant they touched was the total elephant!

E. Yeah, I can see why.

M. So to end this part of our dialogue, a reminder to ourselves that even though we have talked of a sense as being made up of a composite something and a stimulus, it is not as if, for example, a 'visual consciousness' is waiting for a stimulus to come by. The eye—the physical more than the sensitive—may be considered to be in waiting, but *not visual consciousness itself*. What we rather have is an *experience* resulting from a stimulus falling on the retina, and it is this experience that's the visual consciousness, mind consciousness, etc.

E. What a wonderful insight!

M. And so with the other consciousnesses.

E. Yeah. Now I gleam a ray of light.

M. Good. One more thing. A word about the order of the senses. Figure 1A (The fivefold consciousnesses) begins with visual consciousness, and adding 1B (The Three Conditions of Mind Consciousness), ends with mind consciousness. Of the five physical senses, it may appear that we get the most information through our eyes. So beginning with the eye and ending with the body would make sense. But we have seen that the mind is at the back of them all.

E. So you're suggesting that the listing should begin with the mind. Yeah, I remember... Mind is first off the mark!

M. Exactly! And notice again, mindbody, not bodymind.

E. Yeah. Mindbody, not bodymind.

M. Great! But, you know, there is still more to who you are than what we've seen!

E. You gotta be kiddin'... I thought we went rather deep.

M. Yes, we did. But there's more to it than meets the ...eye..., the ear and the nose!

E. Great... I was just beginning to get the hang of things, and now you want to bombard me with more, eh?

M. Well, you wanted to know who you are, didn't you?

E. Of course, of course... I was just kidding. I've been looking for an answer for a long time.

M. OK, then... Let me draw you a figure here to make our life easy. Remember *psychophysique*? Perhaps we could call it 'The Mindbody Tree of Life of Two Branches and Four Twigs' (see Figure 1D).

E. A mouthful alright. But I can relate to some of the terms—the mind and the body branches making up the mindbody tree.

M. So I guess you'd like to know what the four twigs are.

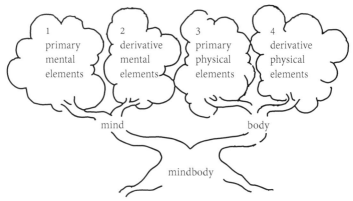

Figure 1D. The Mindbody Tree of Life of Two Branches and Four Twigs

E.   Yeah....

M.   When you come to think of it, it's really very simple. Each branch has a 'primary element' (twigs 1 and 3) and something derived from it, or 'derivative element' (twigs 2 and 4). That's to say each branch has both a primary and a derivative element. Twigs 1 and 2 are the mind branch's twigs, and twigs 3 and 4 are the body branch's twigs. Just as we think of fingers when we say hand. Hand means nothing without fingers, and fingers mean nothing without hand.

E.   Again that necessary, and reciprocal, relationship. Quite straightforward it looks.

⚛ *Scientific Concepts*

1.18   Mind = primary mental elements + mental derivatives.

1.19   Body = primary physical elements + physical derivatives.

M.   Good. Let's have some more fun. Let's see what comes under the primary and the derivative categories... branches and twigs with leaves and all!

E.   I'm with ya all the way!

NOTES, REFLECTIONS & QUERIES

1.4 Summary

1. I'm a mindbody, plain and simple. This means, I have a mind and I have a body, the two working in synchrony.

2. But mind is in charge.

3. This mind is really my sixth sense; so I have not just five senses.

4. It also means that there's no such thing as ESP.

5. For any of the six senses to work, there has to be a working physical sense, a working sensitive sense and a stimulus.

6. This means that the stimulus is part of consciousness and not outside of it.

7. Mind, or consciousness, pervades the whole body, except hair and nails.

NOTES, REFLECTIONS & QUERIES

DIALOGUE TWO

ON YOUR MIND'S STAGE

Now, the mind is the most elusive of all physiological concepts, its secrets locked within the biological black boxes of our brain. Uncovering the contents of these neurological treasure chests is one of the last challenges left to modern medicine.

... our approach to the study of the mind must be to dissect out specific components of behaviour and ability that are well-defined... Overall personality... comprises enormously complicated attributes that will be influenced by many different genes, and by the environment, in ways that cannot be sorted out one at a time...

Walter Bodmer and Robin McKie,
The Book of Man[12]

---

12. Bodmer & McKie, pp.126, 143-4.

2.1 Here Come the Actors

M. To make it easier to conceptualize, let's change our metaphor. Let's think of a drama or ballet performance.

E. If that helps.

M. Here then is a chart that lays out in detail the drama of who you are *psychologically*.

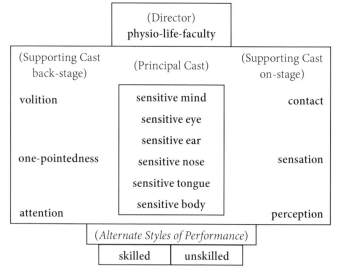

Figure 2A. Buddha's analysis of the Psychological You as cast in a ballet

E. Wow, in the form of a human body even—head, feet and all. A full cast alright. There's even a Director! And nice imagery, too.

M. Yes, it sums up all of you... and me, psychological you and me that is.

E.   You could've fooled me!

M.   Now the mind's ballet, if you will, the psychological drama, is staged by the principal cast (centre), the *primary mental elements.*

E.   *Yes., the* six senses, in step with, can I say, the prima ballerina, the mind!

M.   Perfect. The primary actors, of course, have their supporting cast, *mental derivatives.* To the right are the *on-stage* supporting cast, and to the left are the *back-stage* ones.

E.   I noticed that.

M.   Let me now talk about each member of the onstage and back-stage cast. We noted earlier that for there to be visual consciousness, the image of this page, for example, has to fall on the retina. 'Fall' is the word. That's what's meant by *contact*. To give another example, for your body to know whether the water in the shower is hot or cold, the water, or even before that, the heat or the cold generated by it, has to touch you. Same thing with the ear, and so on.

E.   Fair enough...

M.   *So what* happens when the water hits you in the shower? "Freezing", you'll cry out if it's too cold. Or "Ouch" if hot. Or "Just right". This is what is meant by the second on-stage element, *sensation*. It's the message sent to the brain as a result of the contact. This is the very first level of being aware of something out there.

E.   Touching a hot stove I suppose would be another example.

M.   Indeed. So the point is that for there to be any type of awareness, and eventual consciousness—visual, aural, nasal, lingual, tactile or mental, there has to be contact, and then sensation. Every time.

E. And following sensation, there's *perception*. Do you mean as in 'see', 'hear', smell, etc.?

M. Precisely. These three are, then, sort of the frontmen, frontwomen. But, of course, there's a whole lot of behind-the-scenes activity going on as well. For example, we might come to a decision about what we've made contact with—to either like it or dislike it. We see a beautiful sunset as we stroll towards the lake, and decide that it is beautiful, and decide to like it. If, on the other hand, we see dead fish floating, killed by pollution, we'll jiggle our noses and walk away. We come to the decision not to like it. That's what *volition* is all about.

E. Is the point, then, that we go through this liking-disliking routine with every sense, every time?

M. You got it. Think about it. Can you remember one time (under normal circumstances, such as when you're not on drugs or in meditation) when you made no decision about something you encountered?

E. Well, I can't think offhand... Can I sit on it?

M. Sure. In the meantime, let's go on to the next back-stage element, *one-pointedness*. What does that word mean to you?

E. Perhaps having your mind on one thing?

M. Yes...in order to make that like-dislike decision, you've got to focus on what's coming in—form, sound, smell, etc., one at a time, and exclusively. And that is all one-pointedness is.

E. Makes sense.

M. Now to keep the focus, you need to pay *attention*, right?

E. Which is the last player behind-the-scene.

M. Yes. And notice that every time one or more of the principal actors appear on stage, both types of supporting cast come to play their role. Hence they are together called the *universals*, the always-present.

E. Seems to make sense again.

M. Yes. *Universals* are characterized in texts as being '*common-to-all-minds*'.

E. You mean whenever one or more of the six senses come to be activated?

M. You got it! Now, if the always-present cast makes up the trunk of the body (in Figure 2A), do you notice that the figure has feet, too, labeled *skilled* and *unskilled*?

E. Yes. You show them as 'alternative styles of performance'. What role do they play in this drama?

M. Well, when an actor, or dancer, is at his/her best, both the dancer and the performance can be said to be 'skilled'. When it's poorer, then we have an 'unskilled' dancer and performance.

E. I can go along with that.

M. Now notice that unlike the principal and the supporting cast that are always present, skilled and unskilled never appear together.

E. So they're mutually exclusive.

M. Exactly. They're therefore called *particulars*.

E. Makes sense. So there're these two types.

M. Exactly.

E. But what's this head—*psycho-life-faculty*, you call the Director.

M. Let me begin with an ironic disclaimer—that by the label 'director', I don't mean something in charge, operating behind the scenes, or anything like that. That's the last impression I want to leave with you. So in that sense it's a misnomer.

E.   So why use it?

M.   Only because I wanted to place it in the context of the ballet metaphor—to show that it's different from all the rest, the other individual components.

E.   You want to say a bit more.

M.   Yes, perhaps a better way, to continue the ballet metaphor, is to see it as the floor, as it were, upon which they all—universals and particulars—perform!

E.   So it supports rather than directs.

M.   That's a good way of understanding it. Yes, support. The floor is not part of the ballet, but yet without it, there would be no ballet.

E.   However, I still don't get a full sense of what's meant by it.

M.   Let me help you. The Pali-English dictionary renders it to English as *vitality*.[13] So we could say that without it, there would be none of the other elements.

E.   OK... Keep going.

M.   Texts say it co-originates with life, and is co-terminous with death.

E.   So it covers the whole life span.

M.   Yes. Comparing a sentient being with a plant, we can say the psycho-life-faculty is the basis, the psychological basis, of what keeps us alive. It's the psychological process involved in breathing, in our mobility. It's this vitality, this life faculty, this life element if you like, that makes the difference between say, a sentient being and a plant.

---

13.   Davids & Stede, 1979.

E.   I'm with you.

M.   Perhaps the ordinary English word 'life' should help us—'life' as in that famous *double entendre*, "Is life worth living? It depends on the liver.".

E.   I see.

M.   Or as in "What's the purpose of life?" or "A baby's life is one mass of happiness.".

E.   I'm beginning to get the sense now. So can we say life here means just 'being human'?

M.   That seems reasonable.

E.   But why list it then?

M.   Good question. I've often wondered myself. But, I believe, it's to ensure that nothing that pertains to being human is left out.

E.   It's to be comprehensive, then.

M.   Seems so, doesn't it. But psycho-life-faculty doesn't seem to have any other function other than just to keep life going! Which is why it's called a *'faculty'*.

E.   You know what comes to my mind?

M.   No, what?

E.   A university faculty. A faculty 'comes to be' when the first professor is appointed, and 'ceases to be' when the last one is fired and there are no more faculty members.

M.   We make a great team, don't we?

E.   If you say so!

M.   We've sought to understand the different elements of our psychological make-up in the form of a ballet or play, right?

E. Right.

M. So another way of understanding the concept of 'life faculty' may be to think of it as 'the play', or 'the ballet', itself.

E. How do you mean?

M. Well, let's say we're at the theatre to see a play. So when does the play begin?

E. When the first actor appears on the stage, wouldn't you say?

M. Yes, or when the first piece of music is played if it has a musical opening, right?

E. I'm with you...

M. Good. Now then, when does the play end?

E. As the last actor leaves the stage, or the last musical note comes to an end.

M. Exactly.

E. Oh, I get it. So you're saying that the life faculty is the same as 'the play' which begins with the first actor and ends with the last.

M. You got it. Now, the play is not the actors, not the music, not the dialogue, not the story line, not the make-up.

E. Yeah, just like the ballet is not the dancers, the dance steps, the music and the story line. But all of them together.

M. Exactly. Yet the play, or the ballet, is different from all these other individual elements.

E. OK, so there has to be the life faculty for the sensitive mind or contact or volition or skilled and unskilled states to appear, but none of these are the life faculty itself.

M. You got it exactly right.

E.   Am I glad I got that one! I was thoroughly confused all right.

M.   A final thought. We talked of the different parts of the cell. But cell life is different from any of its parts.

E.   Yeah, it's evident, isn't it?

⚛ *Scientific Concepts*

2.1   *The 'psychological you' are made up of two groups of elements: 'universals' and 'particulars'.*

2.2   *'Universals' are those that are 'common to all minds'; 'particulars' are those that are sometimes present, sometimes absent.*

2.3   *Universals are broken down into 'primary mental elements' and 'mental derivatives'.*

2.4   *The 'primary mental elements' are: the sensitive mind, the sensitive eye, the sensitive ear, the sensitive nose, the sensitive tongue and the sensitive body.*

2.5   *The 'mental derivatives' are of two types: up-front and behind-the-scenes.*

2.6   *The up-front derivatives are contact, sensation and perception.*

2.7   *The behind-the-scenes ones are volition, one-pointedness and attention.*

2.8   *The particulars are 'skilled' and 'unskilled' states of mind.*

2.9   *The 'psycho-life-faculty', a universal, is the psychological life force at the back of the working of the senses.*

NOTES, REFLECTIONS & QUERIES

2.2 The 17-step Dance

M. We've looked at the workings of the mind, and the body, in relation to their parts. We want to now see how the mind process builds itself into the body process.

E. Oh, that'd be interesting. You want to tell me how?

M. Sure. Let me begin by taking you to the Buddha's analysis of what he calls a *stream of consciousness.*

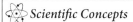 *Scientific Concepts*

2.10 One of Buddha's terms for mind is 'stream of consciousness'.

E. Stream of consciousness? I thought that was a literary style introduced by the existentialists...

M. So it is today. But I believe it came to be a western concept through William James.

E. Psychologist William James?

M. Yes ... one of the two Buddhists who addressed the World Parliament of Religions in Chicago ... Do you know what it is?

E. Wasn't it the first time the different faiths came together on one platform?

M. That's right. In 1893. So one of the Buddhists that addressed the Parliament was the Sinhalese Buddhist Anagarika Dharmapala from Sri Lanka. On a return trip to the US during 1902-4, he visited the psychology class James was teaching at Harvard. Upon seeing him, Professor James invited him to the front, saying, "Take my chair.

You are better equipped to lecture on psychology than I".[14]

E. Oh really? So James was a student of Buddhism.

M. Apparently. But, even before him, a number of others, from around 1850 onwards—David Henry Thoreau among them.

E. Thoreau, too?

M. Yes. Anyway, Chapter Two of James' book, *Psychology: the Briefer Course*, published in 1892, is interestingly titled, 'The stream of consciousness'.

E. How intriguing. So from psychology, it probably made its way into western literary circles.

M. Most likely. But to get back to where we started, Buddha explains a stream of consciousness, whether it is through the eye, ear, nose, tongue, body or mind, in terms of 17 stages. Perhaps we can best show it with another chart:

LCC	Life Continuum Consciousness	
PLCC	Past Life Continuum Consciousness	(01)
LCV	Life Continuum Vibration	(02)
LCA	Life Continuum Arrest	(03)
A	Apprehending	(04)
C	Cognition	(05)
RC	Reception	(06)
IN	Investigation	(07)
D	Determination	(08)
IM	Impulsion	(09-15)
RG	Registration	(16)
RG	Registration	(17)
LCC	Life Continuum Consciousness	

Figure 2B. The 17 stages of a Stream of Consciousness in Buddha's analysis

14. Fields, p.135.

E.   Seventeen stages? You'll walk me through them, won't you?

M.   Certainly! Each of the stages is a *mindmoment*. You'll note that the process both begins and ends with the *life continuum consciousness*. This is simply the *ongoing consciousness*, *before* a stimulus makes contact with any of the six senses. Think of yourself sitting at your computer. Before a single letter is typed, there is first a whole *empty* 'page' is in front of you on the screen. Then, one by one, a single letter, a whole word, line, para, text page, etc. When it's all done, we call it a page, this time with something on it. It's now a printed page. So there was a page at the beginning, and a page at the end. Likewise, everything you've stored in your consciousness, in memory, from conception, up to a given point in time, is the ongoing consciousness.

E.   Oh, that's why it is called the 'life continuum' consciousness?

M.   You got it... So then, one day you take this Life Continuum Consciousness shopping! You're in a bookstore (1). As (2) your eyes scan the shelves, (3) a book catches your eye, because of the particular nature of the stimulus—the way it's displayed, size, colour, lettering, etc. Perhaps (4) you see the title of the book, or the name of the author, and then (5) you say to yourself, "Oh, I know this author and/or title", etc. Now (6) you take the book off the shelf, or if a salesperson is around, she gets it out for you, and gives it to you. You open the book (7) and read through the content, turn a few pages, browse. Next, (8) you decide to buy the book. The cashier is at the front, so you take it to her (9-15). Finally you pay the bill, at which point it becomes part of not only your physical library but also of your mental library (16-17).

E.   An interesting way of putting it. But you want to show the connection?

M.   Sure. Let's try to see the subtle workings behind this process. We begin with scanning the shelves. You haven't figured out as yet what it is that you've seen, but you're aware that your attention has been drawn to a whole slew of stimuli—colour, shape, width, etc., but without making any distinctions between and among them. Your mindbody, your equilibrium, if you like, is slightly disturbed, forming 'ripples', as for example, in the water when a pebble is thrown. Your retina experiences a vibration. This, then, is the *life continuum vibration* (02).

E.   Vibration.

M.   Yes, we can readily see this in relation to the ear. Here's a scientist explaining it: "Traveling into the wide funnel of your outer ear, sound waves reach your brain through a series of *vibrations* that begin in the eardrum. This thin piece of skin causes the hammer bone to *vibrate* and hit the anvil, which activates the stirrup to set up *vibrations* in the fluid of your inner ear [italics added]".[15]

E.   So this vibration in the eye would be my very first general awareness of the presence of books.

M.   Yes, but you still don't know any of them as 'a book'—only as an object that's drawn your attention. In the next mindmoment, your entire mindbody is alerted to the presence, but still barely knowing what the make-up of it is. It is as if the stimulus, namely, colours, shapes, etc. on the shelves, is telling your consciousness, "Freeze! You're under arrest.". This then is *life continuum arrest* (03).

E.   A dramatic way of putting it!

M.   Thank you. It breaks the ongoing consciousness, putting an end, as it were, to the ongoing one and making a new beginning.

E.   So is the next step, then, *apprehending* (04) as I see in the chart?

M.   Yes, it's sort of paying attention.

---

15.   Cumbaa, p.26.

E.   And it would be paying attention to, in our example of books, at the eye sense. Right?

M.   Very good! You're ahead of me! Good. Yes, that would be the eye (meaning here, if you remember, both the sensitive and the physical eye, working in tandem) getting fixated on it, focusing on it. It's like the cop now taking into custody the suspect already under arrest. Then your eyes actually catch a glimpse of the stimulus (one or more), a mindmoment's look as it were. This is *cognition* (05).

E.   OK.

M.   Now you focus on nay, 'welcome' so to speak, one of the books more than others, but without still knowing exactly its nature. This would be *reception* (06).

E.   Seems to make sense.

M.   So now what do you do?

E.   I'll probably take it off the shelf and try to find out who the author is, and what it's all about.

M.   Exactly. And could we call this *investigation* (07)?

E.   Reasonable.

M.   Next, you figure out what it is that you're looking at—that it's a book by so and so and on such and such. This is *determination* (08).

E.   Makes sense.

M.   Everything up to now, let us note, is in the *cognitive* domain.

E.   As opposed to the affective?

M.   Excellent. You must be reading my mind! Yes, now we come to the affective domain. Because at this point, you're no longer merely taking in information *objectively*, in a detached manner. You now actually begin to like or dislike the book.

Here we can see that *volition* has kicked in, if you remember the back-stage cast of the psychological you (Figure 2A).

E. I see.

M. And this is a very important juncture, because it has ramifications for your ongoing consciousness, your future, your liberative chances. In other words, it has a bearing on your *karma*.

E. *Karma*?

M. Yes. Let's understand it for now simply as a consequence of your thoughts and behaviours.

E. So what would be the consequence of my liking what I see?

M. You'll be affected by what you read, wouldn't you, positively, negatively or neutrally?

E. I see.

M. Now, let's say you've determined you like the book. What do you do next?

E. Take it to the cashier I suppose.

M. Of course. Now, this takes more physical time than picking the book off the shelf, right?

E. Yes.

M. So *impulsion*, throwing forward, is shown in the chart as mindmoments 09 to 15. When you take the Pali word for 'impulsion', *javana*, it's even onomatopoeic, making you think of a javelin, like in throwing a javelin, on its way towards the ongoing consciousness!

E. Hm! Interesting the way you put it!

M. The next step would be *registration* (16-17). The title, the author and the book is now part of the store's computer as they are of your *life continuum consciousness* computer!

But you can also think of it as putting it in your library ...of ongoing consciousness! The book is now not only part of your physical library but also of your mental library as well.

E.   Really intriguing!

M.   Now do you have a sense of the 17 stages?

E.   It's truly exciting. Never read such a refined analysis anywhere in western psychology.

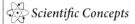 *Scientific Concepts*

2.11   A stimulus goes through 17 stages before becoming part of one's stream of consciousness.

M.   Now here's something else that's exciting. Some recent research, using what's called 'functional magnetic resonance imaging' (or functional MRI), sheds some light on this. Basically, it's a technique to measure the minute changes in the amount of oxygen in blood vessels in the brain.

E.   Yeah, I've heard of it.

M.   Good. Now here're some of the findings: "Above your right eye, an inch or so behind your forehead, sits a remarkable slice of brain tissue, about the size of a postage stamp", the author writes. This is called a 'working memory' by neuroscientists, and given the number 46 in their map of the brain. Now if "you spot a large, round, orange-coloured object with black stripes, your eyes report the sight to Area 46." How do we know? Because this area *lights up*! For a few seconds.[16]

E.   Certainly cognition comes to mind, doesn't it...

M.   Not only that though. What about that whole series—'vibration, arrest, apprehending, cognition ... reception'. Remember that each of them takes a single mindmoment? And note that area 46 lit up not for a single second, but for a *few* seconds.

---

16.   Boyd, 1997.

E. Wow!

M. The two mindmoments following 'reception', if you remember, were 'investigation' and 'determination', right?

E. Aha...

M. To quote the same research findings again, "Your working memory *fishes around* in the files of long-term memory, where such images are stored." How do we know? Again, a "region toward the *back* of the head *glows* when your eyes are busy inspecting an object" [some italics mine]. Now you declare, "It's a basketball.".

E. Okay!

M. Now what did the Buddha say again the second stage was following 'reception'?

E. Let me look at the chart. Oh, yes, determination.

M. Preceded by?

E. Investigation? Wow!! Now isn't that something!

M. That's not all. Listen to this. "If you want to make a *permanent record*—say, of an unfamiliar face—tiny electrical signals flash through a complicated chain of brain cells, called neurons, toward areas *deeper in the brain* dedicated to long-term memory" [italics mine].

E. How could it not remind me of 'impulsion' and 'registration'? This is impossible... I can't believe the Buddha would've had such insights!

M. You said it! Well, today's researchers are so impressed by the working memory that, calling it the 'gateway' to long-term memory, they not only give it the function of "coordinating separate signals coming in from the eyes, ears and nose...", but goes as far as to say that "the working memory may also be the seat of human consciousness"!

E.   I'll be darned! My mind is thrown back to the life continuum consciousness.

M.   Remember us talking about the coordinating function of the mind-sense, coordinating the other five senses? In the scientific research reported here, only eyes, ears and nose are mentioned, because the example given is that of a crying baby who needs a diaper change.

E.   There is certainly no reason why the coordinating couldn't relate to the other senses as well.

M.   You're sharp! From the Buddha's point of view, of course, the scientists are in error on one point—equating just a stamp-size part of the brain as being the 'seat of consciousness' for the entire mindbody. But they're right on if they mean simply that it is (in the language we've been using here) considered the *physical mind* that's at the back of the sensitive mind (i.e., the mind-sense) that coordinates all the senses, including the mind-sense itself.

E.   I can only say, "Wow!". Again. But the Buddha calculates that all this takes 17 mindmoments to happen—from LCC to LCC, door to door.

M.   Yes.

E.   Interesting.... very interesting.... and complex... And you know what that reminds me of?

M.   No, what?

E.   The sixteen frames that make up a single shot in a film.

M.   That's right, isn't it. Never occurred to me.

E.   So for us to get a composite view of a scene, there have to be 16 sub-scenes, moving at a particular speed.

M.   Thank you for making that connection.

E. So what you're saying is that every time our senses become active, we go through this same process...

M. Right on and, of course, there is never a time that the senses aren't active, because the mind-sense, if not the other senses, is on 24-hour duty!

E. And it's always 17 mindmoments between LCC to LCC?

M. Yes. So in a sense, the 17 mindmoments can be seen as an expansion of the on-stage supporting cast—contact, sensation and perception (Figure 2A).

⚛ *Scientific Concepts*

2.12 *Mindmoment = a measurement of time in relation to a stream of consciousness; a unit of time of a stream of consciousness.*

2.13 *Stream of consciousness = a term for a single flow of a mental process made up of 17 mindmoments.*

E. But let me seek a further clarification. Is the number of mindmoments for each stage the same for every mental process?

M. Excellent question... I was hoping you'd ask it... No, they vary, depending on *stimulus strength*. Sometimes not all the stages are present either. Let's say, for example, there's a very faint sound. That would take more than one mindmoment of vibration before arrest would occur. Which means it may end up as a mere vibration, making no impact (registration) on the ongoing consciousness at all.

E. That would explain why we don't remember the face of the person we just passed by on the road. Right?

M. Or the name of the person who was just introduced to us at a party... Texts, in fact, talk about four levels of stimulus intensity: **very great intensity, great intensity, little intensity** and **very little intensity.**

Scientific Concepts

2.14 A stimulus can be of varying intensity, from very little to very great.

NOTES, REFLECTIONS & QUERIES

2.3 Pirouetting with the Un/skillful!

M.   Let's now revisit the mental particulars, shall we, the *alternative types of performance*, the **skilled** and the **unskilled.** You'll probably get a better sense of this if I tell you that sometimes they're translated as morals and immorals.

E.   You mean 'dancing at their best' and 'dancing at their worst' relate to goodness and badness, if we were to say it in plain English.

M.   Exactly the point.

E.   This suggests, then, that there's both goodness and badness in every one of us, as part of our... what was it you said, ... oh yes, sentient condition.

M.   Excellent. You're catching on. Now, however, there's said to be 27 (or 39 by a different count) skilled and only 12 unskilled mindsets.

E.   So more goodness than badness in us!

M.   Indeed. That's why you would find some Buddhist teachers say that we're all Buddhas-in-waiting, *bodhisattas* (Sanskrit: *bodhisattvas*)! Yes, there's more potential good in us than potential bad, considering that each of the good and the bad is an equally powerful force.

E.   That's comforting to hear!

M.   Now here's something I find intriguing in all this. If there is the good and the bad, the moral and the immoral in each of us, that means they're part of sentience. That's to say that we bring them with us when we're born.

E.   So are you trying to say they're genetic?

M. You certainly took it right out of my mouth! Yes. To make the next connection, we could say that morality is genetic.

E. Morality is genetic? Hm, I don't know. I see some fancy footwork here! But isn't morality relative to a culture, group, country, period of time, etc.?

M. That, of course, is the general take on it. But think of it. All human beings can be said to do both good and bad things. What constitutes good and bad may vary in detail, but surely all cultures decry killing, or running away with another's spouse, or stealing, etc.

E. That's true, isn't it?

M. Well, if that's the case, then, by definition, morality is genetic. Indeed each individual may bring with him/her more or less of a propensity in a given trait—say, being kind or cruel. Just like intelligence.

E. Seems reasonable.

M. And, of course, morality being genetic does not suggest an exclusive predeterminism, any more than in intelligence or running speed. Just as intelligence comes to be modified by the environment, and the running speed with appropriate training, so can morality, though inherited, and genetic, be modified.

E. One can certainly make an argument.

M. Good.

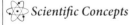 *Scientific Concepts*

2.15 *Both skilled/moral and unskilled/immoral are part of sentience, and hence genetic.*

2.16 *Skilled/moral elements in sentient beings outweigh unskilled/immoral ones.*

E.   But I still need to mull over that one.

M.   Please do. But in the meantime, one other thing we need to note is that the two, skilled and unskilled are mutually exclusive at a given point in time. Not that they don't sometimes walk hand in hand, but that would be in relation to **different** stimuli. For example, a person may be very nice to a friend (skillful) but nasty (unskilled) to another even as s/he is being nice to the friend.

E.   I see. So that's why they're called particulars, and not universals.

 *Scientific Concepts*

2.17   Skilled and unskilled minds may occur with near simultaneity, but only in response to different stimuli.

M.   Exactly. Now, could I leave that with you? Buddha talks of three ways in which our minds could go bananas or stay sane.

Unskilled Consciousness	Skilled Consciousness
attachment	non-attachment
anger, ill will	non-anger, non-ill will
ignorance	non-ignorance

Figure 2C. The three opposing Skilled and Unskilled Mindsets

E.   Now I have a better sense of ...what were the terms.... oh yes, skilled and unskilled. I actually prefer these to moral and immoral because of their other connotations in our western world.

M.   Now let me take you back, if you will, to the 17-stage process of a new stimulus eventually ending up registered as part of the ongoing consciousness. Remember mindmoment number 8, *determination*, following *investigation*!

E.   Aha...

M.   The Buddhian analysis points to a very significant thing happening at the point of determination relating to the skilled and the unskilled.

E.   Whazzat?

M.   Not only does the stream of consciousness figure out what it is that has been inputted (in our example, a book), but also *decides whether you like the book or dislike it*. If you remember, this was the behind-the-scene stagehand 'volition' in Figure 2 A.

E.   What's the connection?

M.   Volition determines the attachment or non-attachment that will arise in your mind.

E.   And this happens with every stimulus.

M.   Exactly. Which sort of confirms the point we've already made—that, as you pointed out, both skilled and unskilled, moral and immoral or good and bad, are part of our sentient condition.

E.   Now I can see it better.

M.   So they're called particulars only in the sense that one can't be both moral and immoral at one and the same time in response to the same stimulus. It's like an on/off switch! But it doesn't mean that a sentient being is *only* moral or only immoral for all time.

E.   That would be commonsensical.

M.   Yeah... But you know what they say about common sense? 'That most uncommon thing called common sense'!

E.   Yeah, I've heard that.

M.   So you can see that what the Buddha says is really deep, but in no sense out of this world. No holy moly stuff with him. Remember, there's nothing for a given person that goes beyond the senses.

E.   Yeah Nothing beyond the senses... OK. So that would be the end of everything psychological in me, right?

M.   For now at least.

E.   But, oh boy, oh boy, how complex can I be!

M.   And me, too, don't forget. You're not going to leave me out of it, are you now?

E.   Of course, not.

M.   So, no Simple Simon you are, for sure!

E.   Certainly not simple. How about Complex Simon?

M.   If that excites you!

E.   Yes, Sirree! Shall we now go to the physical dimension of the mindbody? I can hardly wait...

M.   But before that, you want to try a summary?

E.   Testing me again.

M.   No, myself.

E.   Sure. Alright then, here's the best I can come up with:

2.4 Summary

1. The mind is made up of *primary* and *derivative* elements.

2. The primary elements are the *sensitive mind, sensitive eye, sensitive ear, sensitive nose, sensitive tongue* and *sensitive body*

3. The derivatives are *contact, sensation, perception, volition, one-pointedness, attention, psycho-life-faculty, skilled mind* and *unskilled mind*.

4. All derivatives but the last two are called 'universals' because they're always present; the last two are called particulars because they take turns, and don't appear with every type of mind.

5. The skilled, or moral, mind of sentient beings are double the unskilled or immoral (27 to 39).

6. Morality and immorality, being part of sentience, have a genetic base.

7. Both universals and particulars are not static, but processes.

8. Mind process is called a stream of consciousness.

9. A stream of consciousness is made up of 17 stages, or mindmoments, beginning with *Life Continuum Vibration*. The next of the series are: *Life Continuum Arrest, Apprehending (at the senses), Cognition, Reception, Investigation, Determination, Impulsion* and *Registration*, at which point it becomes part of the *Life Continuum Consciousness*.

10. *Impulsion* takes more than one mindmoment.

11. How many mindmoments are taken at the Impulsion stage is determined by the strength of the stimulus, ranging from *very little intensity* to *very great intensity*.

NOTES, REFLECTIONS & QUERIES

DIALOGUE THREE

AT YOUR BODY SHOP

Being a physicist, I knew that the sand, rocks, water and air around me were made of vibrating molecules and atoms, and that these consisted of particles which interacted with one another by creating and destroying other particles. ...but until that moment I had only experienced it through graphs, diagrams and mathematical theories. As I sat on that beach, my former experiences came to life; I 'saw' cascades of energy coming down from outer space, in which particles were created and destroyed in rhythmic pulses; I 'saw' the atoms of the elements and those of my body participating in this cosmic dance of energy; I felt its rhythm and I 'heard' its sound.

Fritjof Capra, *The Tao of Physics*[17]

---

17. Capra, Preface, p.11.

3.1 Actors with Muscle!

M. Here, then, is a chart, showing all the physical actors, our body parts, on mindbody stage.

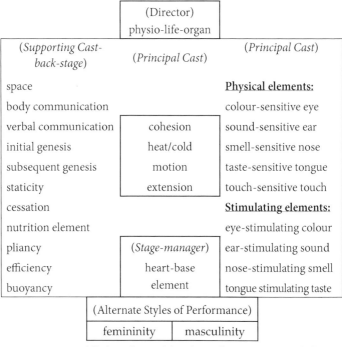

Figure 3A. Buddha's analysis of the Physical You as cast in a ballet

E. Oh, I like your human figure again. It looks even more complex than the mind.

M. Bien sur! Let's begin by noting the same twofold division within *materiality* as in *mentality*—the principal and the supporting cast. Now if they all constitute the *universals*, 'femininity' and 'masculinity' are the *particulars*.

E.   And we'll talk about them in detail, right.

M.   Yes, but first to the main characters which are ...

E.   Cohesion, heat/cold, motion and extension.

M.   Yes. So they're called 'primary materiality'.

E.   Reminds me of the Greeks. Didn't they also have the same four basic materiality?

M.   Yes... but with a difference....

E.   Oh!

M.   For one thing, even though they are labeled 'primary' materiality, they're—unlike, for example, in the Aristotelian understanding—not indivisible. Nor are they unchanging as he thought them to be.

E.   Oh, that's a significant difference.

M.   The term for 'materiality' or 'matter' in Pali, *rūpa*, actually means 'that which has the nature of change'.

E.   I see.

M.   Now materiality is of two levels. The foundational is called 'primary materiality'.

E.   In the physicist's language, *primary materiality* would, I presume, be elementary particles—like protons, quarks, gluons, and so on.

M.   Thanks for making the connection. Buddha also recognizes, however, a higher level, a 'bundle of matter', meaning whatever that is made up of the primary materiality.

E.   Oh, really! This, I suppose, might be *atoms* in physics and *chromosomes* in biology.

M.   Yes, indeed there's a term for atoms in the texts: *anu*, made up of *paramanu*, 'most elementary *anu*'.

E.   Really! So the Buddha recognizes a sub-atomic level? Amazing when you come to think of it. After all, an atom can't be seen with the visible eye.[18] Isn't it said to be a million times smaller than a visible object? And the Buddhist analysis sees even a subtler level. Hm!

M.   Well, as a matter of fact, providing a Buddhist table, a scholar actually calculates the size of the atom to be 10^{10} of a centimeter.[19]

E.   Not very far from the scientist's atom. Isn't their current calculation 10^{-8}?

M.   There you go!

E.   Amazing, that the Buddha could not only envisage the size, with nothing like the instruments of observation available to scientists, but approximates very closely.

M.   But let's not forget. The mind is a sharp instrument.

E.   Well, I certainly can't argue with that!

M.   Now, as I said, as different from the Greeks, the Buddha understands each of these, at whatever level, like everything else in the universe—not as static elements but as ever-changing processes, each with three phases: *coming to be*, *staying put* and *passing away*, or more formally arising, staticity and cessation.

E.   Precisely what science says.

M.   Every hour, scientists have determined, the skin, for example, has to make about one and a half million new cells just to replace all the cells that wear out in this short time span.[20]

E.   That much, and that fast!

18.   Rothman, p.47.
19.   Jayasuriya, p.79.
20.   Cumbaa, p.52.

M. Yes. Something else though. Each of the primary elements contains all the other elements. So, for example, 'cohesion' only means that that's the dominant quality in it. Likewise with the other three.

E. I must say I'm impressed!

M. Now let's try to understand the four primary elements, with the example of a ball of clay (extension). If you heated it up (heat/cold), and got rid of all the water (cohesion), all the sand that makes up the clay would fall apart, blown off internally (motion). And if you took that sand in your palm and let go, it would fly away. But if you added back water, they'd stick together.

E. Straightforward enough.

 Scientific Concepts

3.1 *Materiality is made up of 'primary elements' and 'derivative elements'.*

3.2 *'Primary elements' are fourfold: cohesion, heat/ cold, motion and extension.*

3.3 *Each primary element includes elements of the other three.*

3.4 *'Primary elements' are further divisible to a lower 'most elementary materiality' and combined into a higher 'bundle [of matter]'.*

3.5 *Matter has the quality of change.*

3.6 *Matter has three phases: arising, staticity and cessation.*

3.7 *Physical derivatives are made up of 26 universals and 2 particulars.*

NOTES, REFLECTIONS & QUERIES

3.2 The On-stage Supporting Cast

M. Let's then move on to the on-stage supporting cast in Figure 3A, what the texts call '*directly caused elements*'.

E. I'm with ya.

M. Notice first the two groups: 'physical elements' and 'stimulating elements'.

E. Yes.

M. Remember in our discussion of the psychological process we talked about the three conditions needed for consciousness to become manifested?

E. Let me think here for a moment.... You mean a physical eye, sensitive eye and stimulus?

M. Bravo! Yes. There we dealt with the sensitive elements. Here we deal with their physical counterpart.

E. I see.

M. Now the items under *physical elements*—*colour sensitive eye*, *sound-sensitive ear*, etc.—are simply the physical parts of the body that are sensitive to the stimuli. We should perhaps call what we called 'sensitive eye' (in Figure 2A) the '*mentally sensitive eye*', because what we have here are the *physically* sensitive eye, ear, etc.

E. Yeah, that sounds like a good characterization of the difference.

M. The only thing to note in this physical list is that there's no 'sensitive mind', or 'dharma-sensitive mind', if you remember the dharmas as whatever is the object of the mind.

E. Thanks for drawing my attention to it.

M. The reason for its absence, of course, is obvious.

E. What?

M. Because, by definition, mind is not body.

E. Yes, of course!

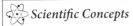 *Scientific Concepts*

3.8 *Each of the sensitive mind, eye, ear, nose and tongue (in the mental domain) has its parallel in the physical domain.*

M. Going down to the next grouping, *stimulating elements*, I know you won't be surprised to note them included under 'material'.

E. Because stimuli are part of our mindbody, as you explained?

M. Excellent! And, of course, form, sound, smell and taste can be physically measured.

E. Of course.

M. The only thing to note in this list of stimulating elements is that there's no counterpart to *touch*. That again is because touch relates to the whole body. But since we're talking of parts of the body, it wouldn't make sense to include it here.

E. I think the ancient scribes have a point.

M. Wind, cold, heat, etc. can, of course, be the stimulating elements for the body, but they are already covered.

E. Mh.

NOTES, REFLECTIONS & QUERIES

3.3 The Back-stage Supporting Cast

M. Can we then look at the *back-stage* supporting cast, the '*indirectly caused elements*'?

E. Let's.

M. Leading the back-stage pack is *space*.

E. Space? As in the concept in physics?

M. Exactly.

E. There can't be space without form, and form without space.

M. Right. This space, however, is not to be understood as a 'thing', texts caution, emphasizing it as a 'non-entity'. So it is called *space concept*. Perhaps a simple definition might be 'the absence of matter'.

E. That would work.

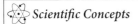 *Scientific Concepts*

3.9   Space is part of materiality, but a non-entity.

M. On to the next two items, *body communication* and *verbal communication* then, shall we—what texts together call the *communicating element*. What does that mean to you?

E. What we're doing now, I guess... exchanging ideas....

M. Well, yes, as process. Through word and body.

E. Oral language and body language as a linguist would put it?

M. Yes. Now oral language, of course, is the marker that distinguishes the human species from all others.

E. But bees, dolphins, chimps and the like communicate, too, don't they?

M. Sure, but in *sounds*, not *language*. So linguistic communication is the unique human marker.

E. I concede defeat!

M. Moving along here, body language, of course, means, gestures, eye contact, physical distance, right?

E. Right.

M. But I'll bet my bottom dollar Buddha meant something more, something far more subtle than that. I believe he meant not just communication between individuals, but also communication *within matter*. Remember, we're talking here about the physical dimensions of you and me, not communication between you and me.

E. An interesting conjecture alright. So let's hear why you say that.

M. We've already said that the mind and the body are in a necessary and reciprocal relationship. We've talked about the mental eye and the physical eye working together to produce visual perception. Likewise with the other senses. These are all forms of communication, wouldn't you say?

E. We could say that.

M. Again, remember the 17 mindmoments? Moving from one to the next would be another form of communication.

E. OK.

M. And finally, at each mindmoment, too, there is communication. I'm talking here about the stages of *beginning, staying put* and *ending*. It's as if each mindmoment somehow 'tells' itself when to commit *hara-kiri*, suicide, also telling the next mindmoment—that's still non-existent, mind you—to be ready to be born! Corny, isn't it?

E. Fascinating!

M. But let's take a more 'living', day to day example which shows
    how the entire mindbody is in communication. Let's say you
    want to go for a walk. First, there is the idea that comes to
    you and then the physical activity of leaving the house and
    walking. Right away we have a connection between mind
    and body. As soon as you think of going for the walk, the
    mind-consciousness immediately puts the relevant parts of
    the body—body muscles, for example, on red alert. 'Ready
    for action'. But as you know, walking involves more than the
    muscles—gait, movement and balance, distance between the
    legs, head position, the mind directing all these. So, 'bodily
    movement' we see, then, is a function of communication.
    And, the entire communication process has to be at work
    throughout the walk.

E. So it's sort of a cybernetic loop, information processing in
    circular fashion.

M. Yeah, exactly. The mindbody is one big information loop
    in action.

E. Mh.

M. Immunologists, too, tell us that the immune system
    works through communication. When a virus attacks,
    the antibodies put the other cells of the system on a war
    footing.

E. That certainly entails communication.

M. Indeed cell biologists tell us that "each cell acts as a
    communication unit...".[21] And, "Every cell has the ability to
    detect signals from its environment".[22] Just like in everyday
    language, they have an encoding system and a decoding
    system, too, and of course, codes! Finally, "[T]o put it

---

21. Kordon, p.34.
22. Kordon, p.24.

briefly, they [cells] can decipher different 'languages' using the same 'alphabet'."[23]

E. Oh yeah?

M. Well, here's how fast such communication takes place. "The incredible organic computer inside your skull can send electrical signals along some of your longer nerves at 300 miles (480 kilometers) per hour".[24]

E. That's eight kilometers (five miles) a minute, and 1.3 km per second! Wow! I can see how the Buddha might have meant by communication more than mere oral and body language. After all, there're no 'words' i.e., language, at the point of conception.

M. Precisely. Didn't I say we have a great team going here!

E. Thanks for the complement.

M. Finally take 'space' and 'materiality'. Again, what we have is communication. Space by definition would be meaningless without form.

E. Makes sense.

 *Scientific Concepts*

3.10   The communicating element of physical you relates not only to verbal and body communication, but also to the cellular level.

M. OK then... On to the next four members of the supporting cast ...what texts collectively call the *phasic element*. Let's get an understanding of them.

E. Let's.

M. Are you happy at this moment?

---

23. Read Kordon's Chapter 1 "The Cell and Its Signals" and Chapter 2 "Decoding & the Cell Messenger System" for details.
24. Cumbaa, p.35.

E. Sure am. Listening to all this interesting stuff!

M. Were you always in this state of happiness?

E. No, not always. That's why I came to you.

M. So you're happy now, but not sometime earlier?

E. Yes.

M. So would it be fair to say that there was a beginning of your happiness and now at this point in time there's a continuation?

E. Yes, that's reasonable.

M. What do you think... is the happiness you now have always going to be there?

E. No, Sirree. I'm sure it will go away sometime. Perhaps even as I leave here.

M. So that means there will be an end to the happiness, right?

E. Right.

M. So you can see, then, there are three phases to anything... On your marks, get set, go! Whether it is happiness or sadness, walking or reading, thinking or dreaming... That's all that's meant by 'phasic element'.

E. Like in communication?

M. Indeed. But what I found fascinating was how it happens even at the quantum level. Here're the words of a distinguished geneticist: "a small fraction of [the] RNA seem[s] to be broken down and degraded almost as soon as it was made".[25]

E. Interesting. That seems to cover all three phases—what you show as *genesis*, *staticity* and *cessation* in your figure.

---

25. Bodmer and McKie, p.44.

M. Quick eye there, eh! Yeah, but you can see the Buddha making a further refinement of the beginning process—*initial* and *subsequent* genesis.

E. I was going to ask about it.

M. Good. We can draw upon cell biology again. Cell division is said to take place in *four* phases, not three: *prophase, metaphase anaphase* and *telophase!*[26]

E. How interesting! Want to tell me what they specifically mean?

M. Well, *prophase*, the Webster's Dictionary defines as "the first stage in mitosis during which the chromatin is formed into chromosomes".

E. *Mitosis* meaning cell division, right?

M. Yes, the most common form of cell division. During this first stage, the dictionary reminds us, "the nuclear chromatin is formed into a long thread which in turn breaks into segments (chromosomes) that are split lengthwise".

E. So there're three things happening—forming into a long thread, breaking up into smaller segments and splitting lengthwise.

M. Exactly. Nuclear, of course, means 'of (or in) the nucleus'.

E. Right. And doesn't chromatin mean some kind of colour— like the chrome in cars?

M. Exactly. It's a "granular protoplasmic substance that readily takes a deep stain".

E. So, it's like coloured grains.

M. But here it's more than just that. A chromatin is said to contain the genes.

---

26. Gray, p.3.

E.   Oh, that does make it a critical part of the process.

M.   Right.

E.   It breaks lengthwise because it's a thread?

M.   You got it. Now we come to the *metaphase*, i.e., the phase between prophase and anaphase.

E.   During which happens what?

M.   Each of the two halves that has gone its way, builds another strand, a complimentary one, using the chemical code inherent to it.

E.   So perhaps when the pair comes together, we have the *nucleus* for a new cell?

M.   Brilliant! In this metaphase, chromosomes, that now come in pairs, come to be arranged along the spindle.

E.   OK. How about the *anaphase*? What happens then?

M.   This is the 'up phase', as it's called, the phase during which the chromosomes already formed moving towards what's called the *centrosome*, or the centre.

E.   So *telophase* would be the final phase.

M.   Exactly. The process of mitosis is now complete, and comes to an end as the parent cell completely divides itself into two cells, each having a nucleus.

E.   So there's an exact scientific parallel. Unbelievable Buddha! That's all I can say!

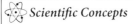 *Scientific Concepts*

3.11   *The phasic element is made up of initial genesis, subsequent genesis, staticity and cessation.*

M. To move along here, let's ask a scientist what the vital properties of a cell's protoplasm are. She'd say, as noted, "motion and nutrition".[27]

E. And my, my! I'm looking at the next item in the list. The Buddha does talk of a *nutrition element*![28] Is that the food we eat?

M. Yes. So the Buddha says, "All sentient beings are food-based". But by food here is meant not only the *ordinary food*—solids and liquids, we buy at the supermarket. Buddha talks about three other kinds of food. One is *contact food*—what we intake through the senses. Basically the stimuli. When you go to a movie, have sex, read a book, work, study, etc., what you are doing is feeding your mindbody through contact. You're contact-feeding!

E. So basically anything I do turns out to be a way of … feeding myself. Without fork and knife!

M. You got it. *Volition food* is the third type. We've already encountered volition in our discussion of the Psychological You (Figure 2A)? Remember the 'determination' stage of consciousness (Figure 2B, #07)? When a stimulus impacts upon one of the senses, you not only determine what it is, but you also determine whether you like it or not. This is volition food—another source of nutrient to the mindbody.

E. Interesting!

M. The last nutrient is *consciousness food*. In our analysis of the 17 mindmoments (Figure 2B), you may remember we noted how they end up as a unit of consciousness. So for that given unit of consciousness, the increasingly complex 17-stage process was the source of food.

---

27. Gray, p.2.
28. While the nutrition element is taken here under the 'back-stage' category because it fits the purposes of our description better, it's to be noted that, in the texts, it's shown as a 'directly caused' element.

E. The foods that keep us going!

>  *Scientific Concepts*
>
> **3.12** *There are 4 foods that feed the body: ordinary food, consciousness food, contact food and volition food.*

M. Let's see what we have next then... Oh yes, *pliancy*, *efficiency* and *buoyancy*. Texts put them under the category *constitutional elements*.

E. OK, So whaddaya mean by 'em?

M. Basically the features of our bodies that allow us for maximum functioning.

E. You want to say more?

M. Chewed gum lately? It's bendable any which way you want.

E. Right.

M. But now think of your body. Can you touch your feet, scratch your back, do a back-loop, wiggle your tongue, move your eyebrows, not to mention fingers and toes, etc.?

E. Yeah, I could. You think I'm an old wug or somethin'?

M. No such word!

E. There is now. Anyway, you know what I mean.

M. Well, of course! You think I'm a wug or somethin'?

E. Ha ha ha!!

M. OK. To get back, you can't, of course, bend the body any ol' way like chewing gum—due to the bone structure—but you can bend it in a number of ways. Ever watched gymnasts at the Olympics? Or ballerinas? Or Indian yogis, or yogi-fake types in circuses? Or Shaolin monks of China who can touch their toes with their nose?! Aren't they unbelievable?

E. Well, if they can touch their toes with their nose!

M. So that would be *pliancy*. When you look at a cell under the microscope, you'll see that no two cells have the same shape. When a cell divides, the second does not necessarily retain the shape of the first. That's why we end up with the nose vertical, the mouth horizontal, the head rounder, fingers long, etc.

E. So what's behind it all is pliancy. And I'm sure you'd argue that pliancy of body also means pliancy of mind.

M. Sharp again! That was precisely what the Buddha says: *pliancy of body* and *pliancy of mind*?

E. I knew it! And there certainly seems to be an element of *efficiency* here as well, as I look at the figure.

M. Yes. Efficiency is what allows our body to do whatever it has to do to maintain its functioning, with maximum precision, minimum effort, timeliness, etc. As soon as the baby is born, she knows how to suckle, or cry. Again, first she's on her back, then she crawls, and later walks. So it's efficiency at work, whether it's suckling, crying, walking or looking through a microscope, or focusing our attention.

E. I suppose efficiency works at the cellular level as well.

M. Indeed. Here's how efficient cells are in their communication:
    Each cell acts as a miniature production facility that can manufacture and manage not only its supply of signals, but also its raw materials and tools, such as the enzymes from which the signals are produced.[29]
Further, a cell
    can control the amount of its reserves of chemical mediators (transmitters) as well as their degree of intensity..., ... dispatch the products that it manufactures.

---

29. Kordon, pp.34-7.

It even has

> *what amounts to a parcel delivery service that is guided by "addresses", by chemical "tags" or "labels", as well as "monitoring units" to control its own communications.*

E.   Gosh! Now isn't that amazing! How much more efficient can a system get?

M.   I'll tell ya... This, then, is what is meant by efficiency. So I believe, efficiency dovetails into pliancy.

E.   And *buoyancy*?

M.   It, of course, means lightness-like a piece of wood on water. Or Neil Armstrong on the moon. Now without buoyancy, we could not walk—pulled down to the ground by gravity, we wouldn't be able to move. Not even our hands or legs. We couldn't swim either.

E.   So no baseball, or soccer or ...

M.   Cricket... Exactly.

E.   So in a sense, *buoyancy, efficiency and pliancy all* literally work hand in glove!

M.   Exactly. And going through the different phases—genesis to cessation, fed by the nutriment elements.

 **Scientific Concepts**

3.13   Pliancy, efficiency and buoyancy are the constitutional elements of our mindbody.

E.   Oh, we nearly forgot the Director and the Stage-manager.

M.   Speak for yourself!

E.   OK, OK!

M.   But let me deal with the Stage-manager first—the *heart-base element.*

E.   Alright.

M.   Simply that, like our eye, ear, etc., we have a physical heart. But while we can live, say, with the loss of eye-sight or hearing, or even smell, taste and touch as in a state of coma, we can't be without a heart.

E.   So you can't be heartless!

M.   Ha ha ha! So anyways, without a heart doing the pumping, there'll be no movement of blood that keeps the body fed.

E.   So I guess we could call it the distributing system. Like the carburetor perhaps?

M.   That's good analogy. Yes, we could say it's the nutrition-distributing system.

E.   I see.

M.   Whether it's at the cellular, placental or the fully-grown level of a human being. Or to put it in the language of anatomy, *vitelline circulation*, *placental circulation* and *complete circulation* of the adult.[30]

E.   Yes... the nutrition-distributing system.

M.   And that's the reason why I like to think of it as the Stage-manager.

E.   Meaning the one who keeps everything and everyone going.

M.   You get the idea.

E.   OK. So, now that we know who the Stage-manager is, can you introduce me to the Director?

M.   Impatient, or what? Oh, but that's the spirit.

E.   Well... So, is *physio-life-organ* (in Figure 3A) the parallel of what we had in the Psychological You chart (Figure 2A)?

---

30.   Gray, p.123.

What was it called, yes, the psycho-life-faculty?

M. Good memory! Exactly. It's indeed the physical counterpart of the psychological process.

E. But I note that you're replacing 'faculty' with 'organ'. Is that a license on your part?

M. Hardly. As a matter of fact, the texts use the term 'organ' to characterize it, I believe to emphasize its physical nature.

E. I see.

M. So we can say that, as in the psychological domain, in the physical domain, too, the life faculty arises at the point of conception and comes to an end at the point of death.

E. Yes, co-generative with conception, co-terminous with death, right?

M. Very good.

E. I'm reminded here of Einstein's theory of relativity. What's now a wave is next a particle... once energy next matter. We seem to be talking of the same phenomenon—once in relation to mind and now in relation to the body.

M. You got it all figured out!

E. Well, we try.

M. Good. Now just as a particle is more tangible, more solid, than a wave, so is the physio-life-organ more tangible than the psycho-life-faculty.

E. It's sort of clear from the term 'organ', isn't it?

M. Just emphasizing the point.

E. In fact I see a variation of Einstein's theory here: once matter (physio-life-organ), next non-matter (psycho-life-organ).

M. Very perceptive, I must say.

E. That's all great, except that I'm still waiting to see what this 'organ' is, in this tangible sense.

M. Now where do you see it placed in the figure?

E. At the head.

M. What's in the head? More to the point, under the skull?

E. The brain?

M. Bull's eye!

E. So it's the brain then that's the physio-life-organ?

M. What do you think? That's my interpretation.

E. Well, I can't grudge the interpretation.

M. Even though the texts don't call it that in this context, a meditational context refers to a 'brain in a skull'.[31]

E. So you're well situated in tradition.

M. Indeed I am. To bring this to a closure then, let me point to the disclaimer I made in relation to the psycho-life-faculty— that we need to think of the physio-life-organ not as 'the power behind' but rather as the one that makes the difference between animal life and plant life.

E. So it can be thought of as the physiological process involved in, say, breathing and mobility?

M. Fantastic. However, in another sense, it can be seen as 'the Director' in the sense that the brain is. It's the brain that sends the messages to all the parts of the body.

E. Of course, of course.

M. But not in the sense of a first cause. Because for the brain

---

31. See fn.45.

to send the messages, there has to be an input, a stimulus, received through one of the senses. So in that sense, the brain is simply *re-acting*, not pro-acting.

E.   Oh, I understand the point you're trying to make.

M.   Oh, good. One final point. Remember the stimulus for the mind-sense?

E.   Well, jog my memory here, would you please?

M.   Just like an object, say a ball, was explained as the stimulus for the eye-sense, thoughts, etc. were shown to be among the stimuli for the mind-sense.

E.   Oh yes, now I remember. You called it..., dharmas.

M.   Excellent. So I would say the physio-life-organ may be seen as the 'seat' of dharmas.

E.   I'm comfortable with it.

⚛ *Scientific Concepts*

3.14   *Physio-life-organ: the physical force at the back of the mindbody.*

M.   Great. But you haven't forgotten that a body has to have feet.

E.   Me? Forget? Never! I see them at the bottom of the figure, *femininity* and *masculinity*.

M.   It's really very simple, isn't it? One is either female or male!

E.   You could've fooled me!!

M.   But, of course, that doesn't mean that one is only male or only female. Just like there is *both* the moral and the immoral in each of us in the psychological you and me, there is both the masculine and the feminine in each of us in the physical domain—the masculine in females and the feminine in the male. Only one is dominant.

E.   Oh, you mean like in the four primary elements.

M.   Exactly. For example, left brain dominance (or "cold logic") is said to be male and right brain dominance (or "warm intuition") female. But yet we know that women are no less intelligent than men are, and that men can intuit, too, and have an emotive life. Perhaps a given culture might not have allowed the flowering of one or the other. Or might have even actively sought to kill them—like crying in public for men in N. America, or western cultures, and showing intellectual skills for women. But that is not to say that emotionality or rationality is not present in each of us, female or male.

E.   And, of course, femininity and masculinity is more than in the brain.

M.   Exactly. But they're called 'particulars' because they're mutually exclusive in the sense of dominance.

⚛ *Scientific Concepts*

3.15   Femininity and masculinity are the 'particulars' in the physical domain of the mindbody.

3.16   Both femininity and masculinity are present in everyone, though one is dominant than the other.

M.   So finally then, we're at the end of the listing...

E.   So, that's all of physical me then. Wow! How complex yet very clear.

M.   Sorry it's taken long, but glad you think so.

E.   I almost feel like saying, "How beautiful!". I mean the Buddha saw all this in his mind's eye—all these subtle things? Wow!

M.   Well, you can see all of them, too, you know!

E.   Me? No, Sirree! Not in a million years.

M.   Ouw, don't be such a pessimist!

E. Just being a realist.

M. But I'm sure the Buddha would say, "If I could do it, anybody could do it."

E. But how?

M. Through meditation.

E. Oh, it'd be a miracle if I could train my mind to see such refinements in my mind's eye.

M. Remember, there are no miracles for the Buddha. Only what's within one's senses. So there's no reason why such subtle perceptions should be beyond you. After all, the Buddha's only research tool was the mind. You only have to set your mind to use your mind!

E. Sure hope you're right, and that someday I can cultivate my mind the way Buddha did.

M. I'm sure you will.

E. Only time will tell!

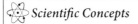 *Scientific Concepts*
3.17   The mind, when trained, is an effective research tool.

M. I've said you're nothing but a mindbody, plain and simple. But now if anyone were to tell you that you are a Simple Simon, or a Simple Simona, you can, again, say, "Hardly. I'm truly a Complex Simon (or Complex Simona)!".

E. Complex all right...

M. Well now, how about a summary—to see how I've done in getting my ideas across.

E. OK. Let me take a crack.

NOTES, REFLECTIONS & QUERIES

3.4 Summary

1. Like in the psychological domain, in the physical domain, too, a sentient being is made up of primary and derivative elements.

2. The four primary elements are cohesion, heat/cold, motion and extension.

3. Twenty-two of the derivatives are 'universal', i.e., always-present, and two are 'particular', i.e., mutually exclusive.

4. The universal derivatives are made up of:
   - 5   physical elements (colour-sensitive eye, sound-sensitive ear, smell-sensitive nose, taste-sensitive tongue and touch-sensitive touch);
   - 4   stimulating elements (eye-stimulating colour, ear-stimulating sound, nose-stimulating smell and tongue-stimulating taste);
   - 1   space element
   - 2   communicating elements
   - 4   phasic elements (initial genesis, subsequent genesis, staticity, cessation)
   - 1   nutrition element
   - 3   constituent elements (pliancy, efficiency and buoyancy)
   - 1   heart-base element, and
   - 1   physical-life-governance.

5. Particular derivatives are 'femininity' and 'masculinity'.

BODY-BUILDING THROUGH MIND-BUILDING THROUGH BODY-BUILDING

... my focused concentration allowed me to penetrate more deeply than ever before into the actuality of my physical being. When the meditation was over, I sat looking about the room at other meditators ... I was filled with a great welling of tenderness for each of them and for all humanity who share with me the condition of this body that is only briefly here, neither solid nor permanent.

Sandy Boucher, *Turning the Wheel*[32]

---

32.   Boucher, p.14.

4.1 Born is Matter

M. We've looked at the makeup of the psychological and the physical domains independently. The element of communication we talked about in relation to the physical reminds us that the two of them, however, need to be understood as an information loop, all parts in each working together.

E. Aha.

M. But, remember, we started out with the assertion that you're a mindbody.

E. I'm with ya.

M. To look at the relationship between mind and body, then, let me turn poetic.

E. Let your poetry be music to my ears!

M. Here then it is:
> *You're what you eat.*
> *You're what you're in heat!*
> *You're what you 'think'.*
> *You're what you ink in a yester wink.*

E. Ooh, what talent you have, grandpa!

M. All the more to make you happy, my dear!

E. OK, so what're you trying to say?

M. The first line you've probably read in health magazines.

E. You mean I'm what I eat?

M. Yes, the body built on food the Buddha calls (*bundle of*) *form/ matter born of nutriment*. So literally "You're what you eat!"

E. OK. But what in heaven's name is *You're what you're in heat!*? You mean as in sexual intercourse?

M. Heavens, no! It refers to the primary materiality heat/cold?

E. Ouw Kay.

M. It is based in the heat dimension of this pair—called 'energy'. Energy, of course, is what you get when you eat, but there's also body energy, psychic energy, etc. which is in-built.

E. OK.

M. All this is *matter born of energy.*

E. Your next line, *You're what you 'think'* reminds me of Descartes: "I think, therefore I am.".

M. Doesn't it? But it both means and doesn't mean that.

E. How do you mean?

M. Remember consciousness food?

E. Aha.

M. Let's return to the 17 mindmoments (Figure 2B) to get a better handle on it. The 16th and the 17th mindmoments, if you remember, were identified with the function of 'registering'. Like a hotel guest. Once the guest registers, she becomes 'part' of the hotel. Likewise, at this end point, the stream of consciousness becomes part of the ongoing consciousness.

E. I remember.

M. But something else happens at this point, too.

E. And what's that?

M. There is now a new unit of matter, resulting from the unit of mind, or consciousness. This is called *matter born of consciousness*!

E.   Oh really? So the mind gives rise to the body. Matter born of consciousness!

M.   Or, if you like, matter born 'of consciousness food'. So if by 'I think' is meant consciousness, then, yes, Descartes is right in here. But as you know, Descartes is the ultimate rationalist, meaning he allows for no feeling or any other sensation. But we've noted how consciousness is very much sense-based—the six senses. The mind sense, of course, includes emotion. Thinking is only part of the process of consciousness. So in that sense, 'think' is not what Descartes thinks!

E.   Your wordplay again.

M.   Mh! To come to the last two lines, *You're what you ink /in a yester wink.*

E.   Yeah. What does that mean?

M.   Remember the mindmoment of 'determination' (08) in the 17-mindmoment series?

E.   What about it?

M.   We noted that at this point, one takes sides; that volition, free-choice if you like, comes into play.

E.   Aha.

M.   This has an immediate reaction—in terms of *karma*. Positive or negative. We 'ink in' a like or dislike in our ongoing consciousness, and this leads to some psychological or physical action—to do or not to do—on our part. You liked that book on the shelf, and you bought it. So liking is 'psychological action' and buying 'physical action'.

E.   Ouw Kay.

M.   So the inking happens as a result of an *earlier* determination. That's the ink of a *yester wink*, 'wink' standing for action. This is *karma*, in its simplest form; It is also Buddha's *volition food*.

E.   Volition food.

M.   Yes. And so we get *matter born of volition/kamma.*

> ⚛ *Scientific Concepts*
>
> **4.1   Matter is born of four sources: nutrition, energy, consciousness and volition.**

E.   I see. So would it be correct to say that matter is partly born of matter (nutrition and energy), and partly of non-matter (consciousness and past kamma)?

M.   Excellent.

E.   And that's what you mean by 'body-building through mind-building'?

M.   Yes. Here we have one of the mind-body connections. We may recall in this connection that Buddha talks of pliancy, efficiency and buoyancy of **both** mind and body.

E.   I remember, yes.

M.   If that's 'body-building through mind-building', there's also right there its reverse process—'mind-building through body-building'.

E.   Because of the reciprocity?

M.   Exactly. You cannot have consciousness, i.e., do mind-building, without physical contact. We saw that in both figures 2A (Psychological You) and 3A (Physical You). In 3A, we noted that the **physical** elements, excited by the stimulating elements, bring about (in 2A) the sensitive mind, sensitive-eye, ear, nose, tongue and body.

E.   And, of course, vice versa.

M.   And, of course, vice versa. Exactly. Now, remember the Buddha calling you names—sentient being, mindbody... Now let me tell ya, he calls ya by something else, too.

E.   He does.

M. Yes. The Five Aggregates.

E.   The Five Aggregates?

M. Yes. Drawing upon the psychological you. According to this name-calling, you're all of *'form-sensation-perception-forces-consciousness'*.

E.   So these are the five aggregates.

M. Right. Notice the first one? Form.

E.   Yeah.

M. 'Sensation' and 'perception' are obvious.

E.   Yes. Because that's what follows contact.

M. 'Forces' is interesting, too. We noted the mindmoments of 'impulsion' among the 17-stage process.

E.   Yes.

M. While here obviously it refers to the psychological domain, it's clearly physical, too. In physics we talk of a 'force'—force of gravity, for example. So here, the force is not only psychological.

E.   I can go along with that.

 *Scientific Concepts*

4.2 A mindbody is made up of 'five aggregates': form, sensation, perception, forces and consciousness.

M. So there, then, is your '...mind-building through body-building', completing the loop.

E.   Yes, I also remember what you said earlier: conditioned by mindbody is consciousness and conditioned by consciousness is mindbody.

M. Fantastic! To be down to earth about it, we can say that when there's no communication between, or among, our many psychological or physical entities, we fall ill—ill in mind, ill in body or ill in both.

NOTES, REFLECTIONS & QUERIES

4.2 The Soulless, Matterless Internet You Are!

M. We've talked of the several constituent parts of which you are made up, and their different functions. However, if you're a bundle of mindmatter, can I also address you as 'Your Majesty MindMatterless'? Or, to completely throw you off, 'Your Majesty a-Mental Materiality'?

E. A what?

M. You remember the mindbody's phasic nature? Consciousness and matter in its three phases—coming to be, staying put for a mindmoment and passing away?

E. So everything changes.

M. This fact of change Buddha calls *anicca,* or impermanence, one of the three 'characteristics' of reality.

E. One of three.

M. Yes. But not realizing this fundamental reality, or perhaps overlooking it, the philosophical thinking of the time of the Buddha held on to the idea of something that doesn't change—giving it the label *atta* (or *atman* in Sanskrit), compliments of Brahma, i.e., Brahminism's Creator God.

E. So it's the same soul idea as in the west.

M. Close, although I'm sure philosophers on both sides of the divide will come up with differences. But, be it *atman* or *soul,* it's said to be created by God, and hence immortal, and hence also unchanging. You can't touch God's work, can you now?

E. Not without offending!

M. However, when we remember the phasic nature of matter, and mind, we have no choice but to conclude that there's nothing that doesn't change. All that cometh to be passeth away.

E. Indeed, indeed. That came out very clearly in our discussion.

M. But we tell ourselves, the Buddha observes, that there's something permanent, something real called 'I', 'me', etc., something to be attached to. This fooling of ourselves itself is **dukkha,** a second characteristic of life.

E. Yeah, I know the term. An existential pain and suffering, right?

M. Or, as a student of Buddhism and a leading American psychiatrist calls it, "an entirely new category of psychopathology".[33] Now the way out of this kind of pain is to realize that there is nothing called a soul, and that 'asoulity', or **anattā**, alone is reality.

E. A what is reality?

M. Asoulity.

E. Do you mean soullessness?

M. Well, that is the more common term. But I want to suggest its absence, as for example, in asexuality (contrast 'sexlessness'), amorality (contrast 'immoralness'), and also to vanguard that absence.

E. I can buy that. So would that be the third characteristic?

M. You got it. So the three characteristics of life are?

E. Let me see here. Oh yes, impermanence, pain and suffering and what was it, yes, asoulity.

M. Wonderful. But let's see if we can establish this last one.

E. Oh, I like that. That way, as the Buddha says, I don't have to take it on your word.

---

33. Engler, p.47.

M. Exactly right. So, let me ask you a question.

E. I'm all ears.

M. What's a 'stream'?

E. A stream? Well, it's water, a bed, and banks. Howzzat?

M. Good. These would be some of the elements. But, of course, there's more to it. It's a *flowing,* too, right?

E. Right.

M. At least we get the appearance of a flow as one molecule of water, or a whole bunch of them, i.e., a current, pushes another.

E. Right.

M. And, then, as you said, there's the bed of the stream.

E. Aha.

M. Now does the bed stay the same even as the flow (of water) changes?

E. Well, doesn't it change, too, depending on how big or small, heavy or light the current is?

M. Exactly. But, in turn, the nature of the current also depends on the extent, the shape, etc. of the bed as well.

E. Bien sur! So you'll perhaps say that the relationship between the current and the bed is a reciprocal one, one determined by the other.

M. You took the words right out of my mouth! Yes, indeed. And wouldn't you say that so are the banks. How wide or narrow they are depends on the flow, which in turn depends on the extent of the bank.

E. Right, of course.

M. Now, is there also not a source for the stream?

E.   You mean like the rain, a mountain, etc.

M.   Exactly. So we can say that the **source** would be a condition for the stream.

E.   No problem there.

M.   So we have now identified three things about the stream. That it's a **process,** that there're **elements** to it, and also **conditions.**

E.   Yeah, that's what we noted.

M.   Well, let me now ask the question. Was/Is there anything other than the elements, conditions and process that's needed to account for a stream?

E.   Let me think for a moment here... I guess not.

M.   So we have now established that the totality of a stream can be explained in terms of elements, conditions and processes, all interconnected.

E.   Well, we couldn't come up with anything else. So, yes.

M.   Let me now ask you, "What's a **plant?**"

E.   Is it OK if I used the same three categories you used relating to the stream.

M.   Let's try it and see.

E.   Well, then, in terms of **elements,** it has leaves, a stem and roots. As a source, or **conditions,** it has a seed, soil, water and sunshine. And there's the **process** of photosynthesis through which the leaves draw upon the sun's rays. There are also the chemical changes in the soil that nourish the roots.

M.   Certainly you pass with flying colours. And is there anything else that's needed to account for a plant?

E.   I can't think of any.

M.   Is there something behind the process, leading it, guiding it, other than the process itself.

E.   I can't see any.

M.   So we establish the same point again—that the totality of a tree can be explained in terms of elements, conditions and processes, all interconnected.

E.   Yes.

M.   Let's then move on to something else. What's a *frog*?

E.   Four legs, a head, eyes, ears, nose, tongue...

M.   Let's not forget the skin. Or the internal organs—brain, stomach, heart, neurons, etc.

E.   Of course, of course.

M.   How about hunger, sex drive, agility?

E.   Yes.

M.   How about communication? Do they have communication?

E.   Croak... croak... croak....

M.   Exactly. Do they have sensations?

E.   I bet they do.

M.   Based in?

E.   Wouldn't we say contact?

M.   So would you go to the extent of saying that, using Buddhist language, that they have the yearning, desire, attachment to live?

E.   Yes, I would say that.

M.   How about the yearning to die... if only to be born again?

E.   Well, that I'm not sure.

M.   OK. Do they have sensual desires?

E.   Wouldn't they want to be in cuddly mud as opposed to dried-up sand?

M.   Any fears?

E.   I'm sure they wouldn't want to get killed.

M.   Yes. And...

E.   And, of course, they're every bit sensuous, if only to procreate.

M.   Do frogs have intelligence?

E.   I suppose it depends on how you define it.

M.   Part of human intelligence is our ability to adapt? Can a frog adapt?

E.   Probably a heck of a lot better than us humans.

M.   Exactly. How about morality? Do they abide by any?

E.   Morality? Hm! Well, if you think of morality as, say, for example, not doing unto others what you'd not want done to you, I'd say yes.

M.   Do they do things that're are harmful to themselves, or others in the species, or beneficial?

E.   Well, again, I don't believe they want to be killed.

M.   Do they do things that are beneficial to themselves?

E.   Mother frogs, more than father frogs, I'm sure, are every bit protective of its young ones as in any other species.

M.   Do frogs experience pain?

E.   Do they ever! I vividly remember my biology lab. When we put a little frog into a jar, and shut the lid, I could see how it was struggling—twisting and jumping—as anyone in pain would, before it died.

M. Just the same way a frog experiences pain, we may surmise it experiences its absence as well, even if we wouldn't be able to say it experiences 'pleasure'.

E. By definition, wouldn't it be? One wouldn't even know what pain is if one doesn't experience what it's not.

M. Do frogs have consciousness?

E. Well, 'frog consciousness', I'm sure, if we understand consciousness the way we've understood human consciousness. I mean, there's a stimulus, say, a fly. It's attracted by it, and then, it decides it likes or dislikes it, and then attacks. So the stimulus, as you well explained, now becomes part of consciousness. So yes, in that sense, I'd say it has a consciousness.

M. Yes, that's what I would've thought, too. Next question. Is change part of their reality?

E. Well, of course. They begin as tadpoles and end up as frogs.

M. So basically, then, frogs share many features with us humans—limbs (eyes, etc.), functions (eating, mating, etc.), characteristics (intelligence, hunger, desires, etc.), and so on.

E. You know what was going through my mind as we were talking?

M. No, what?

E. How much a frog shares with us even metaphysically.

M. You want to say more?

E. Well, they seem to have desire—for food, they have the same fears (say, fear of death), they're subject to change, and morality, in the sense we understood above, is inherent to them!

M. Well, you said it. Let me then ask you: Is there anything other than the elements, conditions and processes that are needed to account for a frog?

E. 'Nope' would have to be my unequivocal answer!

M. Is there anything or something behind the process other than the process itself.

E. I can't see any.

M. So again we establish the same point- that the totality of a frog can be explained in terms of elements, conditions and processes, all interconnected.

E. Good to remind ourselves.

M. Finally, then, what's a *baby*?

E. Oh, that's easy. Head, arms and legs, eyes and ears, crying, feeding, crawling...

M. And internally?

E. Senses...

M. Go on.

E. Fears, pleasures and pain, desire, perception, consciousness.

M. And, change.

E. Yes, change.

M. Here, then, is a figure that shows the comparative features of a river, tree, frog and a baby.

LABEL	STREAM	PLANT	FROG	BABY
CORPOREAL STRUCTURE	Water	Trunk/leaves	Body, legs, etc.	Body, legs, etc.
LIFE MARKER	'Flow'	'Breathing' [by osmosis]	Breathing [psycho-physical]	Breathing [psychophysical]
UNIT OF LIFE	Molecule	Atom	Cell/DNA	Cell/DNA
LIFE SUSTAINER	Water	Nutrients [soil]	Nutrients	Nutrients
PROCESS	Water flow	Energy flow	'Mind' flow	Mind flow
OUTCOME	Changing shape/size	Changing shape/size	Changing shape/size	Changing shape/size

Figure 4A. Features of a stream, plant, frog and baby along the dimensions of structure, life marker, unit of life, life sustainer, process and outcome.

E. Hm, interesting!

M. What similarities and dissimilarities do you see, particularly between a frog and a baby?

E. Well, at the Corporeal level I see none. None in the Life Marker either.

M. But note that 'psycho' in relation to the frog is within single quotes.

E. To show the qualitative difference between a frog mind and a baby mind?

M. Exactly.

E. In terms of the Unit of Life and Life Sustainer, I see no difference.

M. Noting again, however, the qualitative difference.

E. By Outcome (last line), I believe you mean the outcome of the process?

M. You got it.

E. There's no difference there either, of course.

M. Nor in the process, again noting the qualitative difference of the mind flow. And the word 'mind' is in quotes again to point to this.

E. Yes, of course.

M. So the difference between a frog and a baby is qualitative rather than generic.

E. Meaning in kind.

M. Yes. So again we ask the critical question: Is there anything other than the elements, or features, conditions and processes that are needed to account for a baby?

E. Well, the answer has to be 'no'. I mean, if a frog shares all those things with us, and yet we don't say there's anything behind a frog other than the process of living itself, why should it be different in the case of a baby?

M. I rest my case.

E. Case for...?

M. *Asoulity* — that asoulity is the only reality.

E. Oh. So that's where you were leading up to.

M. Yes, that's where I was leading up to. We started by reminding ourselves of the Buddha's teaching that change, not permanence, and asoulity not soulity, constitute reality. Now we have arrived at the same conclusion by looking at the examples of a stream, plant, frog and a baby.

E. Indeed, we have, haven't we?

M. Well let's now see how the Buddha specifically speaks to the issue. Perhaps it's best if I were to quote him directly where he first reviews some of the theories of the soul, making the philosophical rounds of the time:

It [the soul] has been considered as material or immaterial, as limited in size or infinite. Some [i.e., annihilationists] think it exists (only) in the present life, others [eternalists] that it continues to exist in future (lives or existences), or that even if it is not originally of a nature to exist in the future [meaning 'immortal'], it can be made so.

Now how do they envisage a soul? Some envisage it as sensation: my soul is sensation, others not as sensation, as 'not-experiencing.'

Now in the case that the soul is supposed to be sensation, it should be stated whether it is happy, unhappy or neither, since sensations are of these three kinds. These three cannot exist simultaneously on the same occasion. In that case one would have to say when experiencing, for example, a happy sensation, 'this is my soul', but when that sensation ceases one would have to say 'my soul has ceased to exist'.

If on the other hand the soul is envisaged as not sensation, not experiencing, one would have to ask: where experience is completely non-existent, would there be the thought 'I am'? Surely not. Even if the soul is described, not as being sensation, but as having sensations, then if the sensations absolutely ceased [as when a sensation gives way to perception, forces and ultimately consciousness (remember you're the Five Aggregates?)] would there be the thought 'I am this'?

Thus this conception of a soul supposed to be observed (envisaged) in the visible world leads to the conclusion that it is impermanent... having the nature of production and cessation.[34]

E. So the point being?

M. Simply that any conception giving the soul certain properties, such as sensation, happiness, is false since properties themselves are phenomena that are impermanent, originating from conditions. We noted earlier, for example, how it is the condition of an object falling on the retina

34. Dialogues, 11.15 Mahānidāna Sutta.

that results in visual consciousness, and how without this condition, there would be no such consciousness. Likewise, happiness, sadness, or sensation.

E.   I'm beginning to get a sense of what the Buddha meant.

M.   Oh good. But let me add a little more on the topic. The Buddha is in conversation with an enquirer named Potthapada. The discussion is about meditation and how one reaches the 'summit of perception'.

Potthapada: *Is perception the soul of a man, Sir, or is perception one thing, soul another?*

Buddha: *What now, Potthapada, do you assume a soul?*

Potthapada: *I assume a gross soul, Sir, material, made of the four elements [water, fire, wind and earth], feeding on solid food.*

Buddha: *If your soul were gross, Potthapada, material, made of the four elements, feeding on solid food, perception for you would be one thing and soul another...*[35]

Now we may reconstruct the dialogue to bring out the essence of the Buddha's argument.

Potthapada: *Yes, Sir.*

Buddha: *Perception, you agree, occurs as one thing and ceases as another* [remember the phasic quality?]. *But, what do you think, Potthapada, since soul for you is different, can it, too, occur as one thing and cease as another.*

Potthapada: *I think not, Sir.*

Buddha: *So soul would be unchanging, permanent. If perception is changing but soul is not, then the impermanent perception has to be part of the permanent soul. Can such a permanent soul, however, account for a transient phenomenon such as perception?*

---

35.   Dialogues, 1.9 Potthapada Sutta.

Potthapada: *No, Sir. But what if I were to assume a mental soul* [with perfect faculties, here meaning the senses, but called, remember, eye faculty, ear faculty, etc.]?

Buddha: *Do you assume it to be different from perception or the same?*

Potthapada: *Different, Sir.*

Buddha: *What do you say, Potthapada, would it then be the same as in the case of gross soul or different?*

Potthapada: *Same, Sir. Perception comes to be and ceases, while the mental soul, being different from perception, stays unchanged.... May I then propose an 'immaterial soul', Sir, consisting of perception, of which perception is part?*

Buddha: *But if you now think of perception and soul to be the same, would then the soul occur as one and cease as the same or cease as another?*

Potthapada: *As another, Sir.*

Buddha: *If then the soul, like everything else, comes as one and ceases as another, it, too, is conditioned, Potthapada, arising in the presence of conditions, just as visual perception, for example, arises in the presence of the condition of a stimulus.*

E. This dialogue makes things very clear to me. So the Buddha is saying that there is nothing that's unchanging or immortal.

M. Exactly. That's a total fiction of our imagination.

⚛ *Scientific Concepts*

4.3   *Both the mental and the material components of the mindbody have the quality of changeability, or anicca.*

4.4   *Soul is a fiction of the imagination. Asoulity alone is reality.*

E. There's no such thing as a soul. Hm!

M. Perhaps a couple of examples at the pragmatic level to drive the point home here.

E. That'll help.

M. Have you ever cut your finger?

E. I sure have.

M. So who healed it? The doctor?

E. I'm sure I didn't even go to the doctor.

M. Perhaps the medicine?

E. Yeah, you could say that.

M. But medicine is not a doer or person; it can't be the 'doer' of the healing. So does it make sense to say that it did the healing? Or did it merely facilitate the healing?

E. Facilitate I'd say.

M. So if neither the medicine nor the doctor did the healing, who did it?

E. I guess it healed on its own.

M. Now you're talking! So there was *healing*, a process, but *no healer*.

E. That's what it certainly appears to be, doesn't it? Amazing, come to think of it!

M. Let's take even a more common example. We say, "I'm walking". But who is doing the walking? Is it the legs? Is it the body? Or indeed is it the mind? So again, who does the walking?

E. I guess you'd now say the walking does the walking?

M. I couldn't have put it better. I'm sure that's what the Buddha would say, too.

E. Now isn't that something!

M. Sleeping and waking up make the point even better. We can, of course, say, "I'm going to sleep", even though it's a way of fooling ourselves. But we certainly don't say to ourselves *in our sleep*, "I'm going to wake up". Even "I woke up" surely can't mean that we actually did something to wake up.

E. That's true. So it just happens. Awaking does the awaking, and sleeping the sleeping! Huh!

M. Right on! And we get some recent western scientific evidence for the idea of a process without a processor behind it. In a book on consciousness, there's a chapter titled, 'The Illusion of the Mind's 'I''.[36] In it, the author says, "*I exploit [the] idea*[37] *that the self is a construct, a model, a product of conceiving of our organically connected mental life in a certain way.*"[38]

Note the term 'construct' and the phrase 'organically connected mental life'.

E. Yeah., the Buddha's term 'conditions' comes to mind.

M. You're sharp, I must tell you. Anyway, drawing evidence from neurology, the author says, "*the ego is an after-the-fact-construction.*".[39] Further, "*The illusion is that there are two things: on one side, a self, an ego, an 'I', that organizes experience, originates action, and accounts for our unchanging identity as persons, and on the other side, the stream of experience.*" He concludes with the words, citing William James, "*Thoughts themselves are the thinkers.*".

---

36. Flanagan, 1992, ch.9.
37. William James' idea, that is.
38. Flanagan, p.177.
39. Flanagan, p.178, citing James (1892, 68-70).

E.   Thoughts themselves are the thinkers! Hm... Certainly intriguing. Sounds like a nice little title for a book.

M.   Oh, you've been beaten to it, I'm afraid. Mark Epstein has a book with precisely that title: *Thoughts Without a Thinker* (1995). He's a medical doctor, psychotherapist and practicing Buddhist.

E.   Hm. Another book to read...

M.   Will you now allow me to address you as 'Your Majesty MindMatterless'? Or, 'Your Majesty a-Mental Materiality'?

E.   Well, only if I can call you the same.

M.   Why don't you?

E.   'Your Majesty MindMatterless'?

M.   Yes, my child...

E.   'Your Majesty a-Mental Materiality'.

M.   Yes...

E.   Your...

M.   Never mind. I actually like it.

M.   Ha ha ha!

E.   Ha ha ha ha!

 **Scientific Concepts**

4.5   Thought occurs without a thinker, actions without an actor, speech without a speaker.

M.   Let me now bring to your attention how some other scientist characterizes you—simply as a '*self-organizing system*',[40] or even a '*self-organizing living system*'.[41]

---

40. Yovits, Jacobi and Goldstein, 1962.
41. Miller, 1978.

E. Self-organizing because there's no organizer behind the organizing?

M. Exactly.

E. But you want to talk about me as a *living system*!

M. Well, because whether by 'you' we mean the first cell you were at the point of conception, or the psychological you or the physical you made up of the primary and derivative components of the mindbody, or the organs that develop later taken separately, or the total organism of the mindbody, they are all living systems. Simply, they live until they die!

E. That explains the 'living' part, I'd say!

M. And you're a system because at any given level—consciousness, mind or body components, cell, organ, total mindbody—all you are is an interconnected system.

E. Well, of course!

M. And to re-emphasize, the mind is interconnected with the body and vice versa.

E. Yes, *verci vysa*!

M. Ha ha! Seriously, we talked about matter born of consciousness and consciousness born of matter. So what we have again is a give and take, between mind and matter, interconnected.

E. It all makes total sense.

M. Glad we got that out of the way fast.

E. No probs!

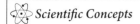 *Scientific Concepts*

4.6   *The mindbody is a system, interconnected in all its parts.*

M. Oh, before we drop the subject, have you been on the internet?

E. I've just got into it.

M. Good. Can I then call you an internet!

E. Me? An internet?

M. Did you note the title of this section?

M. It called you 'The soulless, matterless internet…!'.

E. Oh, izzat what you called me? But why?

M. Well, who controls the internet.

E. No one!

M. Do you see anyone, or anything controlling the mind?

E. Do I see anyone, or anything controlling the mind? Well, from what you've said, no. It appears that when there's a stimulus, or a condition, things just happen.

M. Exactly right. There's nobody in charge. Do you then see any parallels between you (or me) and the internet?

E. Any parallels… hm…

M. Yes. Let me put down something on paper for you.

input	=	stimulus
computer/modem	=	physical eye (ear, nose, etc.)
software	=	sensitive eye (ear, nose, etc.)
internet	=	mindbody

Figure 4B. Comparative features of the Internet and the Mindbody

E. Interesting! Very interesting! The computer/modem is the physical eye, the software is the sensitive eye. Hm!

M. Now here's another way of looking at the parallels.

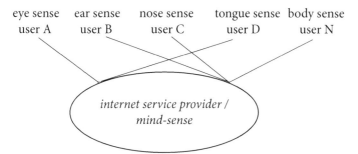

Figure 4C. The Internet Service Provider and Internet Users as
paralleling the Mind-Sense & the other five senses.

E.   Interesting concept again here. Gotta think about it...

M.   Good. Keep thinking. Just as the user wants to access the
internet, the senses want to access the *mindnet*!

E.   And the mind-sense...

M.   You mean mindnet.

E.   Pardon me. The mindnet, if you insist! The mindnet makes
the connections just like the service provider does. Wow, I
never thought of it that way. But I suppose that makes sense,
come to think of it!

M   So the internet could well be another model that both explains,
and supports, the Buddha's understanding of the workings
of consciousness... without a soul. And now to finally bring
closure to our discussion, then, there is, to reiterate, really no
I, no self, no ego, no soul, i.e., *asoulity*, *amentality*, *anattā* is
reality.

E.   I'd be darned!

⚛ *Scientific Concepts*

4.7   The internet is a good model of the soulless mind.

E. Wouldn't you also, I suppose, say *amateriality is* the only reality, too?

M. Gosh! You took it right out of my mouth.

E. It's only logical. Now I understand why I am... what did you say 'a-mental materiality'!

M. More! *A soulless, matterless internet*—that's what you are! So take that!

E. Gee, thanks a lot. Once again, take my humanity away, huh!

M. Not to worry. I'm with ya all the way, the soulless, matterless internet that I am, too!

E. What a laugh!

M. Yes, what a laugh! You don't think Buddha earned the epithet the 'Smiling One' (*mihita*) for nothing!

E. We're in good company, then! But you know what. I'm not any of those what you called me. I still have a name. Me!

M. OK, you.

E. No, me.

M. OK, me.

E. No, not you. Me.

M. OK. You. Me. Whatever.

E. I got ya there, didn't I?

M. Ha ha ha!

E. Ha ha ha!

NOTES, REFLECTIONS & QUERIES

4.3 DNA, Meet the Buddha:
In the Field of Speculation

M. Now for some fun stuff. Some number crunching. Can I invite you to meet your chromosomes, DNA and cells?

E. What?

M. Are you up on your DNA research?

E. Well, not really. Why?

M. It's only a hunch... but I've been intrigued by one fact... How many links are there in a DNA strain?

E. Isn't it 22?

M. Plus 2 for gender, right?

E. Oh, that's right...

M. Now Figure 3A shows the total number of *physical* elements to be 28. If you took away the primaries—cohesion, heat/cold, motion and extension—we're left with 24. Femininity and masculinity are shown as particularistic, meaning that one is either feminine or masculine.

E. Right.

M. So if you took away masculinity and femininity, how many constituent elements are we left with?

M. And they are called universals, meaning common to everybody.

E. Oh my... Are you on to something here or what?

M. I don't know... It's only a hunch. Is it possible that each of the chromosomes in the DNA strand stands for each of these items in Buddha's analysis?

E.   Well, well, well! An intriguing thought indeed.

M.   Isn't it. We certainly know that some of the sciences have come to recognize several of the mindbody features identified by the Buddha. The *sensitive* and the *stimulating elements* have been identified in psychology, physiology and neuroscience; the *heart-base element* in physiology; the *phasic element* in physics and sociology; the *space element* and *buoyancy* in physics; the *intimating element* in cell biology and psycholinguistics; *pliancy* and *efficiency* in cell biology; the *nutriment element* in health sciences.

E.   How true.

M.   So the only elements of the Buddhian mindbody analysis not specifically accounted for in science are the 'psycho-life-faculty' and the 'physio-life-organ'.

E.   Now isn't that something!

M.   But, of course, science does not deny that it's dealing with life, be at the cellular level or the fully grown human being level.

E.   So you're suggesting that what science simply takes for granted, the Buddha includes formally. He is more thorough.

M.   You said it. Remember how the stimulus, taken for granted in science, was included as an essential part of the characterization of consciousness—as for example, a colour in eye-consciousness?

E.   Looks like a parallel alright.

M.   Now, of course, we don't have enough research to show all the functions of each of the links of the DNA chain. But we do know, however, that some illnesses—Alzheimer's disease, sickle cell anemia, for example—are associated with specific chromosomes or genes.[42] We also know that genes contribute

---

42.   Bodmer and McKie, p.144.

to traits such as personality and intellect. So could it be that pliancy, efficiency and buoyancy, for example, and the other physical constituents, or characteristics, identified by the Buddha could also be genetically based?

E. An intriguing thought alright.

M. Mind you, just as "[t]he idea that a single gene could control ... widely varying reactions is ridiculous",[43] it would be outrageous for me to suggest a one-to-one correspondence. But my speculation is—mind you, it's only speculation— that certain specific genes have a hand in life characteristics such as pliancy, efficiency and buoyancy.

E. Certainly a groundbreaking research project for an aspiring PhD candidate!

M. Indeed. One other piece of number crunching. We pointed to the fact that each mindmoment gives rise to an atom. We also noted that there are 17 mindmoments, the 17th being the outcome of the series of 16. Now I don't know what to make of it, and I haven't gone into it, but I find it fascinating that the number of chromosomes in us is "always sixteen"![44]

E. Yeah? Another PhD dissertation alright.

---

43. Bodmer and McKie, p.143.

44. Gray, p.3.

NOTES, REFLECTIONS & QUERIES

4.4 Summary

1. Change, not permanence, is reality.

2. Asoulity is another reality.

3. The mind is comparable to the internet.

OVERALL SUMMARY

M.   Now that we're at the end of a journey, 'Your Mind Matterless Majesty'.

E.   I like the other one better.

M.   OK, 'Your a-Materiality-Mentality Majesty', how about if you were to now give this humble servant a thumbnail sketch of the main points of our long discussion.

E.   Oh, no!

M.   Oh, yes!

E.   You're testing me, aren't you?

M.   No, testing myself to make sure I've got across the points I've been trying to make.

E.   Well, if you put it that way. Alright, then, for whatever it's worth, here we go... looking through my notes. Keeping your fingers crossed?

M.   Sure am.

E.   OK, then here we go.
     1.   *At conception, in my first cell itself, I am a bundle of mindmatter.*
     2.   *The four elements, water, fire, wind and earth, along with space, gave it the physical structure. There was also pliability, efficiency and buoyancy, as the cell got its nutrition from the mother.*
     3.   *But because all of my mind and all of my matter are always changing and nothing stays the same, that first cell reproduced itself to eventually result in an embryo, fetus and plain old me at birth, and thereafter.*

4. 'I' therefore is merely a convenient label, and not to be mistakenly thought of as having a 'soul', unchanging and never-dying.

5. This 'I' continues to live as long as it is fed by the four kinds of food—contact, volition, consciousness and ordinary solid-liquid, maintaining cohesion, which in turn serves as a condition for heat/cold, motion and extension.

6. But this 'I' is nothing but the totality of the sensory inputs turned matter.

7. Hence, I'm only what I sense, and you're what you sense.

M. Bravo! You can now teach a course!

NOTES, REFLECTIONS & QUERIES

SCIENTIFIC CONCEPTS
OF THE BUDDHA

[The number in square brackets refers to the page.]

Dialogue One

1.15 The seat of consciousness is the whole body except hair and nails. [28]

1.16 Your world is nothing but your whole mindbody, nothing more, nothing less! [31]

1.17 Nothing comes from nothing; i.e., all perception is sensory, or sense-based. Hence extra-sensory perception is a fiction. [31]

1.18 Mind = primary mental elements + mental derivatives. [34]

1.19 Body = primary physical elements + physical derivatives. [34]

Dialogue Two

2.1 The 'psychological you' are made up of two groups of elements: 'universals' and 'particulars'. [47]

2.2 'Universals' are those that are 'common to all minds'; 'particulars' are those that are sometimes present, sometimes absent. [47]

2.3 Universals are broken down into 'primary mental elements' and 'mental derivatives'. [47]

2.4 The 'primary mental elements' are: the sensitive mind, the sensitive eye, the sensitive ear, the sensitive nose, the sensitive tongue and the sensitive body. [47]

2.5 The 'mental derivatives' are of two types: up-front and behind-the-scenes. [47]

2.6 The up-front derivatives are contact, sensation and perception. [47]

2.7 The behind-the-scenes ones are volition, one-pointedness and attention. [47]

2.8 The particulars are 'skilled' and 'unskilled' states of mind. [47]

2.9 The 'psycho-life-faculty', a universal, is the psychological life force at the back of the workings of the senses. [47]

2.10 One of Buddha's terms for mind is stream of consciousness. [49]

2.11   A stimulus goes through 17 stages before becoming part of one's stream of consciousness. [55]

2.12   Mindmoment = a measurement of time in relation to a stream of consciousness; a unit of time of a stream of consciousness. [58]

2.13   Stream of consciousness - a term for a single flow of a mental process made up of 17 mindmoments. [58]

2.14   A stimulus can be of varying intensity, from very little to very great. [59]

2.15   Both skilled/moral and unskilled/immoral are part of sentience, and hence genetic. [62]

2.16   Skilled/moral elements in sentient beings out-weigh unskilled/immoral ones. [62]

2.17   Skilled and unskilled minds may occur with near simultaneity, but only in response to different stimuli. [63]

Dialogue Three

3.1   Materiality is made up of 'primary elements' and 'derivative elements'. [73]

3.2   'Primary elements' are fourfold: cohesion, heat/cold, motion and extension. [73]

3.3   Each primary element includes elements of the other three. [73]

3.4   'Primary elements' are further divisible to a lower 'most elementary materiality' and combined into a higher 'bundle [of matter]'. [73]

3.5   Matter has the quality of change. [73]

3.6   Matter has three phases: arising, staticity and cessation. [73]

3.7   Physical derivatives are made up of 26 universals and 2 particulars. [73]

3.8   Each of the sensitive mind, eye, ear, nose and tongue (in the mental domain) has its parallel in the physical domain. [76]

3.9   Space is part of materiality, but a non-entity. [78]

3.10 The communicating element of physical you relates not only to verbal and body communication, but also to the cellular level. [81]

3.11 The phasic element is made up of initial genesis, subsequent genesis, staticity and cessation. [84]

3.12 There are 4 foods that feed the body: ordinary food, consciousness food, contact food and volition food. [86]

3.13 Pliancy, efficiency and buoyancy are the constitutional elements of our mindbody. [88]

3.14 Physio-life-organ: the physical force that's at the back of the mindbody. [92]

3.15 Femininity and masculinity are the 'particulars' in the physical domain of the mindbody. [93]

3.16 Both femininity and masculinity are present in every one, though one is dominant than the other. [93]

3.17 The mind, when trained, is an effective research tool. [94]

Dialogue Four

4.1 Matter is born of four sources: nutrition, energy, consciousness and volition. [101]

4.2 A mindbody is made up of five aggregates: form, sensation, perception, forces and consciousness. [102]

4.3 Both the mental and the material components of the mindbody have the quality of change, or *anicca*. [117]

4.4 Soul is a fiction of the imagination. Asoulity alone is reality. [117]

4.5 Thought occurs without a thinker, actions without an actor, speech without a speaker. [120]

4.6 The mindbody is a system, interconnected in all its parts. [121]

4.7 The internet is a good model of the soulless mind. [123]

A Meditation: Life to Dust

Now you have an answer to the question who you are. So in a sense, you did 'come and see' (see p. v), as the Buddha admonishes. But the dharma, in its explanation and clarification given by me, was inputted into your ongoing consciousness as an *external* stimulus. The Buddha emphasizes again not to accept anything on authority, or even if found in texts. For, there's no way you could know that I or the ancient masters, *Porāṇācariyas*, did not err. Hence the need to pay close attention to the last lines of the Buddha's advice to the householder Kalama (p. v) "...only when you know for yourself...".

To know for yourself. But how? Ask the Buddha. "Through meditation, enquirer". So you heard it, straight from the Buddha. So let's get on with it. Here, then, is a meditation I've found useful to help me arrive at the realization of who I am, *experientially*.

The preparation for this meditation is as for any other. You should have attended to your bodily needs of hunger, elimination, getting dressed, etc. You might want a quiet place, and the best results would be if you did the practice regularly, i.e., same time every day. Preferably just after waking up or just before going to bed. Ideally, you could be seated cross-legged, if only because, research says, that's the best posture for the free flow of the air and energy in the mindbody. But you could just as well sit on a chair, or on a bed. Lying down would not be best at these times, because, especially if you're a beginner, you might tend to fall asleep. Sitting comfortably, then, you would close your eyes, if only to shut out the distraction of other visual stimuli. In this readiness, then, here is the reflection on the 32 constituents of body.

> *In this body, there is head hair, body hair, nails, teeth, skin, flesh, sinews, bones, marrow, kidneys, heart, liver, midriff, spleen, lungs, intestines, mesentery, stomach, feces,*

> *bile, phlegm, pus, blood, sweat, fat, tears, grease, saliva, mucus, synovial fluid, urine and a brain in a skull.*[45]

After each repetition, out loud or in your mind, you would also want to reflect upon other features of the body we have come to know cognitively throughout this dialogue, like pliancy, efficiency and buoyancy of your body, nutritional needs, and any other features that come readily to your mind, without necessarily pushing to see them all.

If this helps you understand who you are physically, then, the following will help you understand who you're emotionally.

> *In this mind are feelings, sensations, perceptions and consciousness, all in a flux.*[46]

After each repetition, out loud or in your mind, you would also want to reflect upon other features of the mind we have encountered throughout this dialogue, but again without necessarily pushing to see them all.

This meditation will not necessarily confirm the total analysis of the mindbody given in the pages of the book, but will let you see the reality in general.

Now to understand sentience in its underlying reality, of asoulity and impermanence, reflect upon how what we call 'life' is the outcome of individual elements, physical and mental, in a process of working together in cooperation with each other, and in a constant flux of coming to be and passing away, subjected to the conditions of nutrition, motion, communication and genes internally, and parents, environment, and the like externally. Now reflect upon the reality of asoulity—that there is nothing outside of elements, process and conditions that are needed to understand life, living, and mindbody.

---

45. Satipaṭṭhāna Sutta, M. 10. Even though the text stops the listing at 'urine', in practice, at least in Sinhalese Buddhism, 'a brain in a skull' is added.
46. This is not from a text, but my own, based in mental components of the Five Aggregates.

Now bringing to mind the joint, or two-sided phenomenon of the psycho-life-faculty and the physio-life-organ we've encountered in our dialogue, reflect upon it. Next imagine that you're lying flat on your back, void of breath. Enjoy the moment!

Now think that you're dead. Experience the moment, with no like or dislike, sadness or disgust, fear or daring. Stay in this as long as is needed to develop the ability to experience this reality with dispassion. And without trepidation.

Now, think of each part of the body, beginning with head hair, body hair, skin and flesh—decaying, and gradually, ending up, as all the body parts go to decay, as a skeleton. Keep a figure of a skeleton at home—buy it at Halloween to help you in this visualization.

Next, going through the same process, visualize that the skeleton, that is you, is no more. All that's left is a pile of bones. Imagine yourself to be those bones.

Now imagine a coat of dust where you're lying. And think of it as yourself now turned to dust! After spending enough time at each step until you become comfortable, and all fear is gone, reflect upon the total process, of how a breathing, living reality has gone through a process of change—coming to be, staying put and passing away—bringing you the experiential realization of impermanence (*anicca*).

The long-term outcome of this meditation, done on a regular basis, would be to fully experience the reality of your mindbody—a temporary manifestation of temporary phenomena! Nothing more, nothing less!!

English-Pali Glossary, for the Really Bold!

Analyst	vibhajjāvādin
Anger	dosa
Apprehending at a sense	[-]dvārāvajjana
Arising	uppāda
Asoulity (soullessness)	anattā
Atom	aṇu/paramāṇu
Attachment	rāga, taṅhā
Attention	manasikāra
Aural consciousness	sota viññāṇa
Bodily consciousness	kaya viññāna
Body	kāya
Born of consciousness	cittaja
" of energy	utuja
" of karma	kammaja
" of nutriment	āhāraja
Brain	matthalunga
Buddha-in-waiting	bodhisatta
Bundle	kalāpa
Bundle of matter	rūpa kalāpa
Buoyancy	lahutā
of the body	kāya 1.
of the mind	citta 1.
Cessation	bhaṇga
Changeability	anicca
Characteristic	lakkhaṇa
Cognition	viññāṇa, sañcetanā
Communicating Element	viññatti rūpa kalāpa
Bodily-	kāya v.
Verbal-	vacī v.
Composite eye	sasambhāra cakkhu
Condition	paccaya
Conditioned co-origination	paṭicca samuppāda

Configuration	saṇṭhāna
Consciousness	viññāṇa, citta, mano
Consciousness food	viññāṇāhāra
Contact [= stimulation]	phassa
Contact Food	phassāhāra
Determination	voṭṭhapana
Directly caused (elements)	nipphanna rūpa
Door	dvāra
Mind -	manodvāra
Body -	kāyadvāra
Word -	vacīdvāra
Efficiency	kammaññatā
of the body	kāya k.
of the mind	citta k.
Element	bhūta rūpa
Embryo [see also 'fetus']	kalala rūpa
Energy	oja
Exit consciousness	cuti citta
Eye-sense, eye consciousness	cakkhu viññāṇa
Eye-door-path	cakkhu-dvāra vīthi
Faculty of life	jivitindriya
(see also 'psycho-life- faculty, physio-life-organ')	
Femininity	itthibhāva
Fetus [see also 'embryo']	kalala rūpa
Five-aggregates	pañcakkhandha
Food	āhara
Consciousness -	viññāṇāhāra
Contact -	phassāhāra
Ordinary -	kabalinkāhāra
Volition -	kammāhāra
Forces	samkhāra
Form	rūpa, santhāna
Gender element	bhāva rūpa
Genesis	uppāda
Greed	lobha

Heart-base Element	hadaya rūpa
Heat/cold	tejo
Ignorance	moha, avijjā
Ill will	dosa
Impermanence	anicca
Impulsion	javana
Indirectly caused (elements)	anipphanna rūpa
Initial genesis	upacaya
Investigation	santīraṇa
Life	jīvita
Life Continuum Arrest	bhavāṅgupaccheda
Life Continuum Consciousness	bhavāṅga (citta)
Life Continuum Vibration	bhavāṅga calana
Life faculty/organ	jivitindriya
Life force	samkhāra
Lingual consciousness	jivhā viññāṇa
Masculinity	puṃbhāva
Materiality	rūpa, bhautikatā
Matter	rūpa
Mental construct/object	dhamma, dharma
Mental derivatives	cetasika
Mind	citta, mano, viññāṇa
Mind consciousness (sensitive mind)	manoviññāṇa
Mindbody	nāmarūpa
Mindmoment	cittakkhaṇa
Minisculest primary materiality	paramāṇu
Minute ball	sukhumagoḷaka
Motion	vāyu
Name	nāma
Nasal consciousness	ghāṇa viññāṇa
Non-anger	adosa
Non-attachment	virāga
Non-entity	nijjiva
Non-greed	alobha
Non-ignorance	amoha, vijjā

Nutriment element	oja, āhāra
One-pointedness	ekaggatā
Ongoing consciousness	bhavāṇga citta
Ordinary Food	kabalinkāhāra
Particulars	pakiññaka
Perception	saññā
Physical derivatives	upādaya rūpa
Physical mind	mano
Physio-life-organ	jivitindriya
Pliancy	mudutā
of the body	kāya m.
of the mind	citta m.
Primary materiality	rūpa dhātu
Primary mental elements	citta
Primary physical elements	mahabhūta rūpa
Psycho-life-faculty	jīvita, jīvitindriya
Reception	sampaṭicchanna
Registration	tadālambana
Relinking Consciousness	patisandhi citta
Season	utu
Sensation	vedanā
Sense	indriya, dvāra
Sensitive element	pasāda (rūpa)
Sensitive eye	cakkhu pasāda
- ear (inner ear)	sota pasāda
- nose (inner nose)	ghāṇa pasāda
- tongue (taste buds)	jivhā pasāda
Sensitive mind	
(mind consciousness)	mano viññāṇa
Sentient being	satto
Series	santati
Sex element	bhāva rūpa
Skill	kusala
Skilled (smart) mind	kusala citta
Small embryo	khuddhakagarbha
Smiling One	mihita

Space concept/element	ākāsa paññatti
Staticity	ṭhiti
Stimulating element	gocara rūpa
Stimulus	ārammaṇa
- of great intensity	mahanta ā.
- of little intensity	paritta ā.
- of very great intensity	atimahanta ā.
Stream of consciousness	viññāṇa sota
Subsequent genesis	santati
Suffering	dukkha
Tactile [body] consciousness	kāya viññāṇa
Tactile stimulus	poṭṭhabbārammaṇa
Touch	phassa
Universals (mental)	sabba sādhāraṇa (citta)
Unskilled	akusala
Unskilled (dumb) mind	akusala citta
Visual consciousness	cakkhu viññāṇa
Verbal	vacī
Vitality	jīva
Volition	sañcetanā, samkhāra
Volition Food	manosañcetanāhāra
Word	vācā

Expressions:

All sentient beings are food-based:
  sabbe sattā āharaṭṭhitikā

Conditioned by consciousness is mindbody:
  viññāṇa paccayā nāmarūpaṃ;

Conditioned by mindbody is consciousness:
  nāmarūpa paccayā viññāṇaṃ

BIBLIOGRAPHY

Anguttara Nikáya, 1929, Colombo.

Bodmer, Walter and Robin Mckie, 1994, *The Book of Man*, Viking.

Boucher, Sandy, 1993 (2nd edition), *Turning the Wheel*, Boston: Beacon.

Boyd, Robert, *Toronto Star*, December 7, 1997, p.F8.

Capra, Fritjof, 1983 (2nd edition), *Tao of Physics*, New Science Library.

Cumbaa, Stephen, 1991, *The Bones Book*, NY: Workman.

Davids and Stede, 1979, Pali Text Society's *Pali-English Dictionary*, London: PTS.

Dhammapada.

Dialogues of the Buddha, London: Pali Text Society.

Engler, in Wilber et al, 1986, *Transformations of Consciousness*, New Science Library.

Epstein, Mark, 1995, *thoughts without a thinker*, Basic Books.

Fields, Rick, 1981, *How the Swans Came to the Lake: a narrative history of Buddhism in America*, Boston: Shambala.

Flanagan, Owen, 1992, *Consciousness Reconsidered*, MIT.

Gray, Henry, 1995 (16th edition), *Gray's Anatomy*, Senate.

James, William, 1985 edition, *Psychology: the Briefer Course*, Univ. of Notre Dame Press.

Jayasuriya, W. F., 1963, *The Psychology and Philosophy of Buddhism*, Colombo: YMBA Press.

John, E. Roy, 1976, "How the Brain Works", *Psychology Today*, May.

Kordon, Claude, 1993, *The Language of the Cell.*, NY: McGraw-Hill.

Macy, Joanna, 1991, *Mutual Causality in Buddhism and Systems Theory*, SUNY Press, Buffalo, USA.

Majjhima Nikāya, London: PTS.

Miller, James Grier, 1978, *Living Systems*, McGraw-Hill.

Rothman, Tony, 1995, *Instant Physics*, NY: Fawcett Columbine.

Saṃyutta Nikāya, London: PTS.

Sugunasiri, Suwanda H. J., 1995, "Whole Body, not Heart, the Seat of Consciousness: the Buddha's View", *Philosophy East and West*, 45, 3.

Varela, Francisco J. Evan Thompson, Eleanor Rosch, 1995, *The Embodied Mind*, MIT.

Watanabe, Fumimaro, 1983, *Philosophy and its Development in the Nikāyas and Abhidhamma*, Delhi: Motilal Banarsidass.

Yovits, Marshall C, George T Jacobi and Gordon D Goldstein, 1962, *Self-organizing Systems*, Spartan Books.

INDEX

ABOUT PARIYATTI

Pariyatti is dedicated to providing affordable access to authentic teachings of the Buddha about the Dhamma theory (*pariyatti*) and practice (*paṭipatti*) of Vipassana meditation. A 501(c)(3) nonprofit charitable organization since 2002, Pariyatti is sustained by contributions from individuals who appreciate and want to share the incalculable value of the Dhamma teachings. We invite you to visit www.pariyatti.org to learn about our programs, services, and ways to support publishing and other undertakings.

Pariyatti Publishing Imprints

Vipassana Research Publications (focus on Vipassana as taught by S.N. Goenka in the tradition of Sayagyi U Ba Khin)

BPS Pariyatti Editions (selected titles from the Buddhist Publication Society, copublished by Pariyatti)

MPA Pariyatti Editions (selected titles from the Myanmar Pitaka Association, copublished by Pariyatti)

Pariyatti Digital Editions (audio and video titles, including discourses)

Pariyatti Press (classic titles returned to print and inspirational writing by contemporary authors)

Pariyatti enriches the world by

- disseminating the words of the Buddha,
- providing sustenance for the seeker's journey,
- illuminating the meditator's path.

Made in United States
Troutdale, OR
03/27/2024

18758455R00101